DOWN AND OUT

LABOURING UNDER GLOBAL CAPITALISM

DOWN AND OUT
LABOURING UNDER GLOBAL CAPITALISM

TEXT
JAN BREMAN AND ARVIND N. DAS

PHOTOGRAPHS
RAVI AGARWAL

DESIGN
BRINDA DATTA

OXFORD
UNIVERSITY PRESS

OXFORD
UNIVERSITY PRESS

YMCA Library Building, Jai Singh Road, New Delhi 110 001

Oxford University Press is a department of the University of Oxford. It furthers the
University's objective of excellence in research, scholarship, and education
by publishing worldwide in

Oxford   New York

Athens   Auckland   Bangkok   Bogota   Buenos Aires   Calcutta
Cape Town   Chennai   Dar es Salaam   Delhi   Florence   Hong Kong   Istanbul
Karachi   Kuala Lumpur   Madrid   Melbourne   Mexico City   Mumbai
Nairobi   Paris   Sao Paulo   Singapore   Taipei   Tokyo   Toronto   Warsaw

with associated companies in Berlin Ibadan

Oxford is a registered trade mark of Oxford University Press
in the UK and in certain other countries

Published in India
By Oxford University Press, New Delhi

ISBN 019 565 3041

Typeset by Seapia Graphics, 2204 Sector D II, New Delhi 110 070
Printed by International Print-o-Pack, New Delhi
Published by Manzar Khan, Oxford University Press
YMCA Library Building, Jai Singh Road, New Delhi 110 001

D E D I C A T I O N

DOWN AND OUT is dedicated to the memory of Praful Trivedi and Mohan Patel.

Praful spent his life, all too short, in trying to raise the voice of the poor masses in the state of Gujarat. He became the founding father of JANPATH in Ahmedabad. On this common platform he managed to bring together a wide range of social activists, all engaged at the grassroots in the struggle against the exploitation and oppression of Adivasis, Dalits, child workers and other vulnerable segments in society.

Mohan was born and bred in a milieu suffering from deprivation and discrimination since innumerable generations. He fought his way up to mainstream society the hard way. Yes, he did benefit from some of the facilities set aside for underprivileged people like him. But he always kept looking over his shoulder, conscious of all those less fortunate than he was, but also aware that among those whom he had joined there were many who did not take so kindly to his upward mobility. Partly because of these anxieties his life was cut short at a rather young age.

ACKNOWLEDGEMENTS

We would like to thank the Indo-Dutch Programmes on Alternatives in Development (IDPAD) and the Office of International Relations in the University of Amsterdam, which, along with the Small Funds Project of the Netherlands Embassy in Delhi, aided us in meeting the cost of production of the book.

The branch office of HIVOS in India generously provided funds for its wide distribution.

We are grateful to our friends in the Centre for Social Studies in Surat for their advice and support.

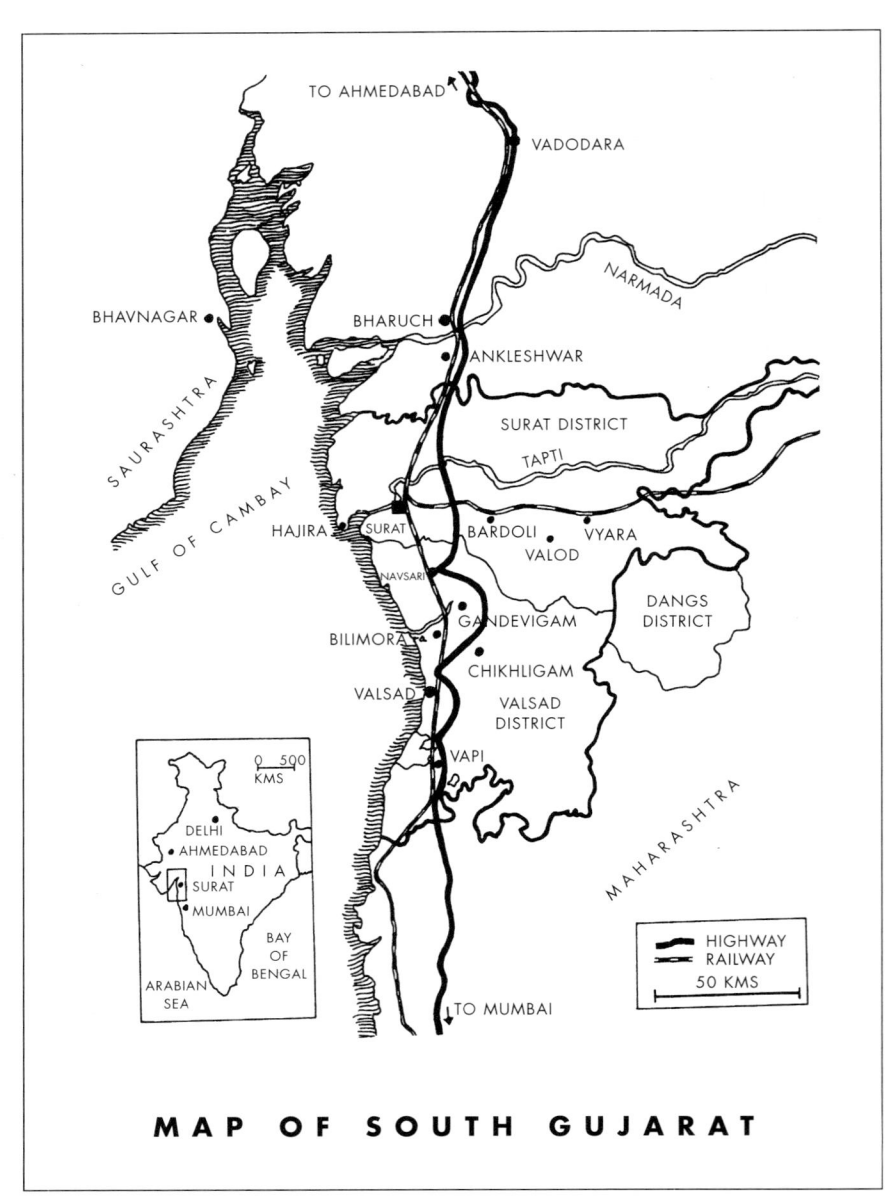

MAP OF SOUTH GUJARAT

C O N T E N T S

1

PROLOGUE

BY JAN BREMAN

The human condition of rural labour was the theme of my first research in India nearly four decades ago. The countryside along the west coast of South Asia's subcontinent became the setting of a long series of investigations, which I started to carry out in the early 1960s and have continued until today, on the life and work of the people stuck at the bottom of the rural economy. In post-colonial India the term 'labour' was understood to refer to industrial work, but for no good reason at all, since the biggest working class ever in world history had a rural identity and was mainly or solely employed in agriculture.

I was ill prepared for the magnitude and intensity of misery that I encountered in the villages of my fieldwork. Born and bred in an European working class neighbourhood and having lived as a young boy through the turmoil of the Second World War, I knew what poverty and oppression meant. But the sub-human subsistence imposed on the landless underclass in my research localities came as a brutal shock. I met men, women and children of the tribal caste of Dublas in their ramshackle hutments, deprived of basic material needs, i.e. sufficient food, adequate shelter and a reasonable state of health. A good number of them were still attached to landowning households in a condition of near-bondage. Sometimes people who had no wherewithal at all ate earth to still their hunger in the slack season of the agrarian cycle. I saw not only children going around naked but also adults who had no dry clothes to replace their wet rags when they came home from the fields on monsoon days. And I heard tales of how women were sexually molested by males in the households to which they were attached.

I used to describe these agonies, so vividly imprinted on the mind of a young man, in letters sent home. My old mother, who barely managed to hold a pen — she had not gone beyond three years of primary schooling and even that very haphazardly — responded with a single letter, one of the few ever written by her, in which she commented that however bad things were at present for these poor Dublas, the next generation would surely be much better off. She knew what she was talking about. Mem belonged to a family of boatmen and had lost four of her eleven siblings while still young, due to such common incidents as drowning, malaria and cholera, while sailing the rivers and canals of the Netherlands with her parents in the early years of the twentieth century. She had seen the like of the Dublas when their barge went to fetch peat from the tribe of diggers working in the wilds of the country. Their grubby children with matted hair and the womenfolk, who did not even have wooden clogs to wear in the bogs, were shy of intruders and hid in the thatched, windowless huts which served this lot as their abode. All this was so similar to my findings in the shoddy quarters of the Dublas on the margins of the village, seemingly far more than a stone's throw away from civilisation. The stories I related about this underclass of mankind did more than just stir my mother's memory. She told me how, after the stark misery of her youth, life slowly started to get better. Her parents' barge was much too small to provide sleeping and eating room for all the children at the same time, and while only eleven years old she was sent off to work as a maid servant in the big city. In her wanderings through the streets and going from one job to another she found at the age of sixteen a partner in my father, who also hailed from poor country-boating stock. The young couple went ashore to join the working class and to establish a home and a family of their own. Reflecting late in life on her early married years she told me about how they could eventually afford to rent a house with tap water and a privy, about getting electricity (which my father used sparingly right until his death), about

their first sewing machine and radio set, all in the 1920s. The next two decades the process of improvement halted, to pick up again in the late 1940s. But then in rapid succession came such major material comforts as the washing machine, refrigerator, TV and telephone. Social provisions such as health insurance, child allowance, old age pension and a senior citizen's apartment after my father's retirement from his job as postman, were all welfare state benefits that dignified their labour class lifestyle. My mother was certain that all these advances in well-being would be shared as a matter of course by future generations of the working poor in my Indian villages. And she had a strong case, arguing that the immense progress experienced by her generation had materialized, and unevenly so, within barely half a

At a much earlier age than these two youngsters, sons and daughters of bargemen worked along with their parents. Although prohibited by law, child labour was prevalent in the first decades of the twentieth century. This photograph was taken in 1931 near Amsterdam

century. Why, then despair about the emancipation of Dublas from the abysmal state of exploitation and semi-captivitiy in which I had found them?

My mother's vision differed little from the design drafted by India's statesmen around the mid-twentieth century for the destiny of the nation and its citizens. Freedom from alien rule was meant to be followed by liberation from the deprived and servile conditions in which the landpoor and landless peasants continued to live. How were those promises, made in the course and context of the freedom struggle, going to be fulfilled? To ease the pressure on agrarian resources was urgently necessary and took priority over all other strategies. The option of overseas migration, still open to the redundant workforce thrown out of the European countryside during the nineteenth century, was proscribed to Asian peasants from the start. Under colonialism, coolies had been sent to faraway destinations as indentured labour for the new mining and plantation settlements that came up as part of globalizing capitalism. A century later, however, their countrymen were not welcome as free citizens to settle in sparsely populated regions of the world. The label of 'economic refugees' has a long and coloured history.

In post-colonial India the imperative need to raise agricultural production and productivity precluded any radical land reform. In spite of repeated pledges that property rights would be handed over to the actual tillers of the fields, policy-makers now argued that there was simply not enough surplus land available to include the vast mass of agricultural labourers in whatever redistribution took place. As a result, long-standing inequalities in the village community were hardly touched. To keep intact the social hierarchy at the grassroots level was what the caste of peasant owners, who now dominated the rural economy, wanted to safeguard. As progressive farmers, they became both the backbone and the main beneficiaries of the Green Revolution which, from the 1960s onwards accelerated the pace of capitalism in agriculture. This breakthrough in a stagnating countryside did little, of course, to solve the social question of how to raise a huge and largely superfluous landless workforce above the poverty line. To realize this goal the political leadership insisted that the agrarian–rural mode of production, the societal framework on the South Asian subcontinent since time immemorial, would soon fade away to be replaced by an industrial–urban way of life. The drive towards industrialization had the additional charm of pre-empting persistent claims for a more thorough restructuring of the agrarian hierarchy than the piecemeal reforms that had belatedly been carried out. Spokesmen for the down-and-out in the rural economy could be placated with the suggestion that, instead of increasing the deadweight at the bottom of the rural order by parcelling out tiny plots that were bound to remain uneconomic land holdings, their underprivileged clientele would find a much brighter future in the multitude of urban factories that would soon spring up.

In this way the modern industrial worker was identified as the heralding force in the transition to urban class society, in contrast to the peasant–cultivator who called the shots in the on-going caste order of the countryside. The only hitch to this rosy line of reasoning was that, according to prominent observers, the 'underemployed' labour reserve showed little inclination to move out of India's hinterlands at their own free will. Their backward and unproductive behaviour to stick to their rustic existence was explained by the thesis of immobility. A typical example of this view, highly popular in policy circles, was Gunnar Myrdal's statement in his influential three-volume *Asian Drama* that 'the poorer the people, the stronger the barriers to migration; poverty squeezes the margin for risk-taking, blunts the incentive to try new things, and rigidifies all restraints upon initiative' (1968, III: 2140). Lacking the capabilities of economic man the rural poor would literally have to be driven to the industries in the cities, for their own good of course.

How could I reconcile this policy scenario with the state of affairs in my fieldwork niches in Gujarat? The big landowners were no longer interested in engaging most of their erstwhile bonded labourers fulltime. With rare exceptions, however, the Dublas were never considered eligible for employment in the modern factories of Mumbai or other big cities. Immediately after Independence India had less than 10 million industrial workers, of whom fewer than half were subjected to a factorised labour regime. This class, hailed as the vanguard of industrialism, which in the wishful thinking of post-colonial statemasters, was charged with the glorious task of shaping the economy of the future, had expanded little in the previous 50 years and has not grown very rapidly during the second half of this century.

In 1969 the National Commission on Labour reported on the social profile of the workforce found in the regular and protected employ of modern industrial enterprises: firmly rooted in the urban milieu, originating in the petty bourgeoisie, educated and upwardly mobile.

The fairly well-paid jobs held by this privileged segment were far beyond the scope of the reserve army of labour made up by the landpoor and landless masses in the countryside. They lacked the social and educational qualifications needed to enter the technologically advanced plants which, in any case, contributed much less to economic growth than had been hoped. Only a few decades after the birth of the new nation the path designed for the future was already in need of agonizing reappraisal. If not totally aborted, the route to industrial–urban society and the contemporaneous rise of the welfare state which had become the hallmark of European development, would take much longer than my mother, although backed up by India's politicians and planners, had anticipated.

The Dublas of Gujarat, like many other contingents of the huge reserve army of labour in different parts of the subcontinent, got trapped in a kind of intermediate regime between agriculture, which could no longer absorb them, and capital-intensive industry which did not want them. But were they in a state of immobility as had also been predicted? Most certainly not. In fact, one cannot begin to understand the resilience of the peasantry without recognizing the lack of fixitiy inherent to their mode of production in past and present. The very first fieldwork which I carried out in the early 1960s included trips to the brickfields on the outskirts of Mumbai, where the landpoor and landless families from my Gujarat village found seasonal employment after the harvest. The expanding circuits of communication and fast improvements in road transport have certainly made 'work migration' more voluminous in recent times. The flow is two-way, not only movement out of but also within the countryside. Massive wage labour circulation — between country and town as well as rural to rural, for either long or short periods and, last but not least, a never-ending switch between various sectors of the economy — is expressive of a situation in which the working poor have to constantly stay on the move in order to survive. They were pushed out of agriculture and the village economy, but only few have managed to settle more permanently wherever they went and whatever they did.

What has been the impact of this intermediate labour regime on the state of deep poverty which marked the life of the rural underclass four decades ago? A first important finding is that the poor have gradually become less poor. A repeat study of the same villages carried out from 1986 to 1991, a quarter of a century after my initial fieldwork, enabled me to report on signs of progress in the Dubla

localities. Their food intake was more stable and the quality of what they ate was better. Adults had now more clothes than the ones which covered their bodies and most children no longer went around stark naked. Housing conditions had somewhat improved and I found less people in chronic ill health. Part of the youngsters now went to primary school, irregularly but on most days that they were in the village and when the teacher happened to turn up. The rich may have become much richer, also in the countryside, but the hopeful message is that by and large the poor have not become poorer. No doubt, life could hardly have been more degrading for the down and out whom I met in the early 1960s. To my conclusion that things have somewhat improved since then I have to add immediately that the progress has been anything but dramatic. The large majority of the landpoor and landless are still far below the poverty line, fixed rather arbitrarily at having less than one dollar per head per day to spend on basic needs. So what causes me to be moderately optimistic about further improvements in their condition? The steady diversification of the economy during the last four decades has created not only more space for rural labour to move around but has also strengthened their bargaining position vis-à-vis their many bosses in and out of agriculture. Due to the widening and lengthening of the labour market, more employment opportunities have become available, even if on short-term contracts only. For some time at least real wages rose and this change for the better resulted in lessening the degree of deep poverty. More significant, however, than this mild relief in material discomfort has been the rise of a new social consciousness in the milieu of the landless.

The Dublas nowadays are adverse to be called Dublas, which has the meaning of weaklings in colloquial parlance, but insist on being addressed by the name that Gandhi gave them in the days of the freedom struggle. But even their entitlement as Halpatis, workers of the plough, seems to have become outdated. The unwillingness of the younger generation to continue to work in the village fields should be seen as resistance to the subordination imposed on them by the main landowning class. Labour circulation causes new misery and dependency, as the photos in this book illustrate, but it is also a way out of the exploitation and the remnants of agrarian bondage that have become intolerable for the large masses which have to make a living by selling their labour power. Their sense of deprivation has actually increased because, although still very much down and out at the bottom of the economy, these people are acutely aware of their exclusion from the wealth that they generate locally as well as far away from home. There can be little doubt that this swelling tide of assertion to insist on a fairer share in the distribution of prosperity is going to find political expression, sooner rather than later.

This book portrays the life and labour of footloose workers in the informal compartments of the urban and rural economy in the southern parts of Gujarat. The region is in the centre of a zone along the coast of west India, stretching from Mumbai to Ahmedabad, and is reputed for its high growth rates from the late 1960s onwards. How high? We can only guess at the answer because in the prevailing climate of informalising economic production, the dynamics of labour nor capital are well documented or registered in reliable statistics. The progress made in Surat city and its hinterland is very much in evidence, however, and that fortunate state has much to do with *kalu* or number *be*, black money passing along both covert and overt conduits in quantities that are hard to believe. Money which has no legal standing takes care of two-thirds of the cash flow and the only 'taxes' on about half of the total value manufactured consists of payments in the nature of fraud, bribery and corruption. The public good is not very visible in Surat. The huge underbelly of the economy is the operational terrain for criminalized politics and prostituted bureaucracies, cashing-in on the richesse of wheeler-dealers. Our pictures do not aim at bringing out these features but focus firmly on the world of work and labour, although the two sides should be seen and understood in tandem.

The intermediate labour regime which has emerged in the region out of my long-standing research is a clear case of the type of dynamics strongly promoted by international financial agencies for Third World countries: more production and higher productivity but all that without labour legislation and with the abolition of whatever government machinery had been set up for that purpose in the past; no minimum wages and protected employment; no regulation of work conditions and

hardly any trade unions daring to mobilize and unite the fragmented workforce. The policies of structural adjustment had a strong presence in Surat city and its hinterlands even before they became a precondition for more World Bank and IMF loans. The landscape of Gujarat could be advertised as a training ground for planners and politicians worldwide. Here they can learn how to reshape urban as well as rural work and employment modalities in line with the undiluted and unfettered capitalism that has become the essence of the informal sector economy. But they will then also have to come to terms with the crucial question, so far left begging, of how to respond to the claims of the DOWN and OUT for inclusion, not as a mere factor of production, a commodity to be hired and fired at will, but as people allowed to live in human dignity, free from poverty and oppression.

▶ **A brickmoulder takes a short break. He has been working since midnight. It is now 8 a.m. and he still has six more hours to go**

2

INTRODUCTION

Like many disciplines, labour studies too have suffered from stereotyping. For many decades, the prototype of 'labour' was the male worker toiling on assembly lines in factories: the powerful and yet simplified image presented by Charlie Chaplin in his classic *Modern Times*. Over time, other elements got added to the stereotype: that of the unionised, organised working class struggling essentially for its own interests. From that grew the picture of the 'labour aristocrat', the well-paid economistically-oriented worker who had lost his proletarian character, abdicated his responsibility in mobilising others in society to bring about political change.

The problem with that image was that it was only partly correct. A section of the working class had indeed got immersed in mere economism and had become smug — in some colonial countries it had even been co-opted by the bourgeoisie in joining the 'national' project of exploiting the colonies and sharing the spoils. But there was much about the working class that was taken for granted. Since sections of it were organised, it was assumed that all of it was unionised. Since some workers in colonial countries with welfare states had achieved

▶ **The ubiquitous tea-boy toiling in restaurants, road-side stalls and canteens is hardly ever taken to be part of the 'working class'. And yet his labour is a significant part of the service sector**

relative prosperity, it was taken for granted that exploitation of labour itself had ceased. This simple-minded, partial and unreal idea of labour led to disillusionment with the working class itself.

There was an intellectual and even political backlash against the organised, unionised economistic working class. By the early 1970s, not only students of labour but even organisations like the World Bank had discovered 'unorganised labour' and the informal sector as a counter-phenomenon to the so-called 'labour aristocracy'. It was suddenly recognised that there is an entire stratum of labour that exists but whose existence is rarely acknowledged. It was as if labour studies had once again gone back to taking note of the 'tinker, tailor, soldier, sailor, rich man, poor man, beggar man, thief' who had been written about in the early years of the Industrial Revolution and generally taken for granted subsequently. In fact it was re-discovered that there are many in the labouring poor — peddlers and prostitutes, plumbers and painters, street vendors and domestic servants — and many, many others who service the elite in many ways but are beyond the social pale. They build and sustain economies but are seen as being the perennial outsiders. In the discourse of development they are pushed down from the text to the footnote and in the actual management of the economy they are relegated to what has been designated as its innocuous sounding informal sector.

This division of workers into sectors — formal and informal — creates an artificial duality. Indeed, even as the concept of the informal sector was advanced, its critique also developed. The critique was on many grounds. The most significant criticism of the concept was that it was confined, by and large, only to the urban economy, as if the informal sector did not have an existence beyond the city limits and did not exist in the rural milieu. Another criticism was that the concept was often used descriptively, with an analytical laziness that did not seek clarity about the size, relationships and dynamics of the informal sector. And finally, perhaps to distinguish this sector from the formal or 'organised' workforce, there was over-emphasis on self-employment in the informal sector, again on the false assumption that 'employment' went along with unionisation and organisation. Thus, through the creation of this artificial duality, the working class was segmented into

◄ **A plumber and painter wait for work. Having some skills and means of production other than mere hands and feet add substantially to the going wage rate for pavement artisans**

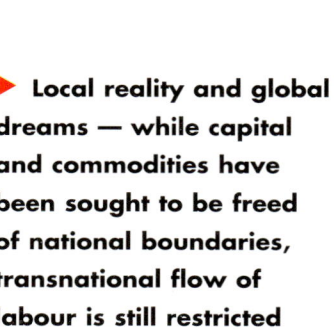

▶ **Local reality and global dreams — while capital and commodities have been sought to be freed of national boundaries, transnational flow of labour is still restricted**

the organised and unorganised, the formal and the informal, and was fragmented into urban and rural, male and female, industrial and agricultural and other clear-cut 'black and white' categories.

There is in fact a continuum in the workforce, ranging from the miserable rag-picker to the relatively well-off organised sector high-tech factory worker. In fact, by making pertinent but simplistic dichotomies, we tend to lose sight of multiple identities and ambiguities in the vast landscape of labour. There are of course many differences across the spectrum of various forms and types of labour but it is also important to note the commonalities and essentialities of labour, particularly in

these 'post-industrial' times in a 'globalised' world.

Globalisation has created a situation where production has been separated from the markets: commodities can be produced in one place and consumed in quite another place. The result is also that there is no relationship at all between the lives of the consumers of such commodities and their producers: diamonds, for instance, may be forever, as the famous advertisement informs buyers, but diamond-polishers are not; their working lives are nasty, often brutish and invariably short. Hence, globalisation means that goldsmiths and diamond-polishers labour in hovels in Surat while the jewellery and

gems that they produce glitter in faraway lands, those who add value getting only an infinitesimal share of the value added.

But then, like the formal sector, which has its counterpart in the informal sector, globalisation too has its complement in localisation. There is a great deal of production and trade which takes place in the local context, at a petty level, in ways that could be characterised 'pre-industrial' if they were not also integrally part of the modern, industrial economy. Indeed, modernity and industrialism have ugly underbellies: the so-called informal economy. It is an economy based on scrounging, on under-paying, on over-working, on misery and on absolute poverty. It is based on de-humanising the labouring poor.

And yet, the real point of the informal economy is not poverty. In that respect, the term 'labouring poor' is somewhat misleading since its focus too is on poverty rather than on the labour that, even in its degraded condition, is as integral to the economy as modern industry. In fact such labour, and such capital too, are the base on which the edifices of commerce and capital are erected.

This organic and mutually sustaining relationship between the informal and formal sectors is quite different from the assumptions about capitalism and development that were made in the first decades after Independence. The development paradigm that became dominant then suggested a major shift would soon take place in India from a rural–agrarian to an urban–industrial type of existence. In the course of that transformation the condition of poverty in which people were accustomed to live, then considered to be the essential 'Asian drama' caused by low levels of production and productivity, was supposed to end. It was to give way to improved levels of living expressed in better food, health, education and housing, in short a life of human decency and dignity. Although social and economic progress has indeed been made during the last half century, nevertheless more people than ever before find themselves at the dawn

of a new millennium in a state of immense poverty.

It is important, however, to reiterate that the deprivation and degradation of the poor cannot be understood as the inevitable outcome of stagnation and backwardness. Their origin lies in the politics and policies of the development process itself. For instance, the deprivation of the people portrayed in this book does not result from

unemployment or defects in their labour power. Contrary to the idea that poverty is a manifestation of economic redundancy, the down and out produce wealth from which they however remain excluded as beneficiaries. Most of them are the working poor who continue to live in a state of misery and oppression because of the low wages paid for long hours of work.

Occupational multiplicity — doing as many jobs as can be available, and often simultaneously — and cyclical mobility — moving from work sites to work sites almost seasonally — are, in any event, prominent features of the life of the working poor. However, the combined process of urbanisation and factory-based industrialisation, which over a time span of about two centuries transformed the character of western societies, seems to take a different shape in Third World countries such as India. Here even migration is a two-way process. When people go away, they do not necessarily stay away: there is a circulation of labour. Most resourceless workers are pushed out of the village only to be pushed

Migrant workers in the cities usually live in slums in miserable conditions and without basic amenities even as they are employed in the construction industry to build offices and homes

back again after several months or a couple of years in a repetitive drift. Besides, the nature of production itself makes the village a point of arrival as well as of departure. Against those who are driven out there are others who are driven in to work as sugarcane cutters employed by agro-industries or in other rural-based industries such as stone quarries or brick kilns.

Thus, instead of documenting the poverty of

underdevelopment, this book presents images of people producing wealth, creating growth and sustaining development without themselves sharing justly and fairly in the prosperity and well-being that they have significantly increased. It is significant that both within the nation-state as well as worldwide the disparities in all ranks of life separating the privileged from the dis-privileged have further sharpened. The poor in some instances might have become less poor than earlier, but the rich have become immensely richer. And while equality has become a commoditised article of faith, according to the UNDP and other such agencies, inequality has increased and intensified.

There is no equality even among the working poor. Nor is there social homogeneity. Even the solidarity created by trade union and political action often does not exist. The working people are nowhere near becoming a class for itself; they do not even constitute a class in itself. The working masses floating around at the bottom of the urban economy of Surat and its rural hinterland, for instance, have highly diverse social identities and are also highly segmented in their very mode of employment. The differentiation within their ranks is very marked: powerloom operators and diamond cutters and polishers earn five or six times more than brick kiln workers and sugarcane cutters.

But overriding these heterogeneities is the vulnerability of the workforce not incorporated into the formal sector of the economy at large. Constituting not less than 80 per cent of all labour outside agriculture, they are neither organised by trade unions nor protected by state legislation. They lack the social security that dignifies life and labour.

It is clear that labour that is down and out is at the beck and call of capital, utilised and discarded with an apparently arbitrary economic logic. However, the simple, if also cruel, fact is that the very high profit margins in the informal sector circuit have a logic of their own. These super-profits are, of course, neither spent in making adequate payments to the massive workforce and in improving conditions of work and increasing productivity. Nor are portions of such wealth available to the state as taxes to be used for public spending. Surat had already been made into a haven for owners of capital long before the currently fashionable globalisation–privatisation–liberalisation orthodoxy became the order of the day in South Asia. It is a type of capitalist development that results in much higher rates of accumulation than are recorded in official statistics. It has been estimated that about 60 per cent of the total cash flow in Surat city falls in the category of *kalu*, i.e. 'black' money. There is a straightforward relationship between the small and shallow tax basis and Surat's reputation of being one of the dirtiest and most epidemic-prone cities in India, lacking in the most basic public amenities. It was only after the so-called plague broke out some years ago that sustained efforts were made to clean up the streets and remove garbage heaps. However, there was a downside to even this: under the guise of beautifying the urban space, the working poor were evicted from their open-air shelters and driven to niches out of the public sight. It is another matter that within a matter of weeks they were back in the streets again because of the need felt by a large variety of employers to have an ample supply of cheap labour instantly. Constantly available at easy hailing distance, this is labour that is present but not necessarily 'visible'.

The visibility not only of labour but also of capital is low in the informal sector economy. Labour in this sector is necessarily mobile, coming and going according to the demands of production; it is, therefore, often ignored altogether or, at best, treated as a temporary incursion in the urban habitat. But much of the business in the informal sector is unstable, shifting, even shifty: massive trade in diamonds is, for instance, carried out almost surreptitiously. One of the consequences of this relatively invisible informal sector economy is that it is based outside the purview of the State. Paying wages lower than the legal minimum, carrying out production in conditions worse than prescribed under law, evading taxation and flouting municipal regulations — all these create

conditions for massive accumulation and super-profits. At the same time, laws intended to protect labour and the environment are flouted with impunity and funds meant for public spending are appropriated for private purposes by politicians and bureaucrats high and low in the hierarchy of power and administration.

While the working poor are included in the labour process, they are excluded from their rightful place as citizens in mainstream society. Consequently, the working poor are seen as a dangerous instead of a redundant class: dangerous because a wily, evasive, erratic kind of behaviour is ascribed to them. This view of the labouring poor derives from the Social Darwinism that was fashionable in the 1860s, premised not only on the idea of 'the survival of the fittest' but also based on the axiomatic assumption that the poor were physically, intellectually and morally inferior and indeed 'unfit'. In some respects that idea is making a comeback today. In any event, the 'middle-class householder' is never comfortable with a mobile workforce, one whose movements cannot be regulated. In spite of the fact that a specific type of capital needs precisely that kind of labour, there is still a lurking idea that such workers resist the work regime to which they are exposed and are apt to avoid discipline imposed on them. It is assumed that casual work, contract labour and self-employment are modalities which they prefer because these strategies allow them to opt out temporarily, to retreat in niches of their own.

And in some respects that is true too: workers in the de-humanised informal sector do manage to carve out little autonomous spaces for themselves, spaces within which they seek to assert their dignity. This they do by turning precisely the informal and casual nature of their employment and the unregulated nature of their non-work time. The constraints imposed by capital are turned into small freedoms by labour.

The specific form that post-industrialisation has taken in India towards the end of the twentieth century has resulted in large numbers of factories being closed down. This is especially so in the once vibrant textile industry; aged, smokeless and now useless chimneys dot the urban skyline as vestigial remains of a once-upon-a-time enterprise; decline in the influence of trade unions and other organisations of workers go hand in hand with mass unemployment and casualisation of labour. All this has, in many respects, reversed the processes of production itself — from being carried out in factories to once again being fragmented into manufactories. Indeed, globalisation has also meant increased 'informalisation'. The consequences are severe for the labour process as well as for the labouring people. This book seeks to portray the life and labour of precisely such workers.

3

THE VILLAGE

The stereotype of the ageless and unchanging Indian village is just that — a mere stereotype. The fact is that the Indian village is constantly changing and in most cases, the village is neither autonomous nor isolated, nor has it ever been so.

The most stereotypical image of the village is one of an idyllic, self-sufficient peasant community engaged principally in agrarian-cum-craft production. The picture is one of a relatively undifferentiated population and of rustic simplicity, even if it is also one of stagnation.

The problem is that the picture is not true.

Today, not only has the picture of rural self-sufficiency been proved to have been unreal, agriculture is no longer the major economic activity in many villages. In some cases, towns have physically taken over the village space: the urban scenario looms over the rural horizon. In such cases, if agriculture is carried out at all, it is in the shadow of the cities and caters to the new markets that the cities have created. In other cases too, even if agriculture remains the predominant economic activity and towns and cities are still physically remote, the market has moved ever so close. The landscape of peasant production, so

characteristic of Asia at large,.from generation to generation, has gone forever to be replaced by a rapidly expanding urban–industrial order of sorts.

There is also increasing differentiation within the village reflecting the differentiation in society at large. The village has the same discrepancies in terms of money and power that is a feature of society in general. Migration too does not necessarily mitigate inequality. Indeed, it has been argued that migration is 'the mother and father of inequality: it is inequality that initiates it and it ends with greater inequality'. The fact is that both the poor and the rich migrate and thus the social hierarchy at the local level is incorporated and reconstructed in the wider market.

Most villages are now integrally connected to the market and the market significantly influences their existence. The subordination of villages to market forces operating on the basis of remote control has drastically altered lifestyles at the top as well as the bottom of the social order.

◀ **There is no end to easy slogans such as 'Garibi Hatao' but still the hope for a better future remains. It is also noticeable that tribal women do not tie their *saris* any longer between their legs but have started wearing their dress in a more 'dignified' fashion**

The market itself has many dimensions.

It relates, of course, to consumer goods. Branded products are on sale even in the pathetic little shops in the poorest village hamlets and the persuasive influence of advertising has started becoming manifest even in the rural hinterland, not just to sell goods but also to bring politics to the people. The hidden persuader is no longer hidden! The market includes within it not only the branded and unbranded goods that the village imports and consumes but also such commodities that it exports and sells. The grains, the fruits and the vegetables that the village produces principally for sale outside are part of the relationship between the village and the ubiquitous market.

But the market also encompasses within it other elements of the economy. Among those are land, credit and labour.

Land is bought and sold, mortgaged and redeemed with an intensity that demolishes the myth of the stagnant village economy. And the rural and peri-urban land market is brisk not only because of agriculture but also because of the needs for habitation, transport and production. The village serves as location for people — people who stay there and people who come and go. The land market, therefore, acquires many elements that extend from production to reproduction.

Similarly, credit too takes many forms. It appears in the village through institutonal finance provided by banks and also through usury indulged in by ruthless moneylenders who perpetuate bonded labour. The surprising familiarity of the illiterate Indian villager with the complicated numerical formulae of interest rates is part of the heritage

▼ **The consumption expenditure of rural labour households has not increased significantly in the last two decades. In fact, the proportion of expenditure on food has remained static at 68.6 per cent. This stark fact is reflected in the pathetic shops in most villages**

of an economy based for centuries on a complex, vigorous, if also extremely exploitative, credit market. But the most important connection is through the operation of the market for labour.

An early assumption in political economy about the relationship between capital and labour was that labour would at least be paid a subsistence wage, and subsistence was defined as the cost of maintaining the labourer as well as providing for its replacement. However, in almost all of the informal sector and even much of the formal sector, the wages actually paid are far below the cost of subsistence. Workers live sub-human lives, often as 'bachelor'

migrants, at their work sites and the reproduction of labour takes place far away in the village. Thus, the village subsidises capital and commerce and it, in turn, gets affected by them.

For one, village after village is today strangely devoid of able-bodied adult men: they have all gone away to work elsewhere. The population of the village comprises the old, the infirm and the young. Many of the elders have themselves passed through the grinding mills of capital, which squeezed out their labour power. They live out the remainder of their lives on memories. Other men have been so brutalised by their experiences that they seek to escape the world

▶ **Since Independence many schemes have been launched to improve housing in villages. The new houses have been poorly designed and built with inappropriate materials. They are monuments to bureaucratic insensitivity and many such houses stand unoccupied while the poor continue to live in their huts**

through an alocoholic haze. Their drunkenness increases the double burden of the women, who, true to their reproductive role, try to get the male labour power back on their feet.

The infirm are of no use to the cruel labour market, which works on the cynical pretence that there is no such thing as a free lunch. And the young, nurturing themselves and smaller siblings, are still in preparation to join the reserve army of labour, waiting for capital to call on the reserve at its convenience.

Devoid of much of its 'manpower', many such villages are unable to sustain a vigorous and productive agriculture since ploughing is still a male preserve, ritually taboo for women. In any case, the fact that many of its 'working women' also have to migrate to towns and cities makes even animal husbandry fairly unproductive with pathetic cattle somehow meeting the meagre needs of the village.

Since literacy does not necessarily lead to improvement in the economic condition of the landpoor, there is no premium put on education and such schools as exist do not make a major mark. Housing schemes too initiated 'from above' have hardly had a positive impact: the new houses built under different schemes have proved largely to be unsuitable and, in many instances, even unusable. Villagers, therefore, often prefer their traditional habitat, even though it is often lacking in basic amenities like adequate drinking water, sewerage and sanitation. In this respect, it appears that the more the village changes, the more it remains the same.

And yet the village has changed in major ways during the last five decades. Agriculture is no longer always the leading source of employment and income. Diversification of the rural economy means

It was said that most Indian women migrate at least once — when they get married. Migration for paid work was otherwise considered to be the prerogative of men. Recent changing economic and social factors have created situations where, like labouring men, many women are also forced to be constantly on the move

that a sizeable part of the total workforce has shifted to other sectors: industry, construction, transport, trade and services. Indeed, one of the consequences of this is that an economic continuum has been established between town and country in this respect. Urban work opportunities draw labour to towns, leading to rural–urban migration. At the same time, both labour-intensive seasonal agricultural operations, like sugarcane cutting, and the many varieties of non-agricultural rural work — in brick kilns, stone quarries, salt pans or even in the village proper in activities like basket-weaving, etc. —

require that a village-to-village movement of workers also takes place. Thus, instead of the village witnessing an outright exodus, it experiences the circulation of labour. The village becomes both the point of departure for emigrants and the point of arrival for temporary immigrants.

The economic and social status of the migrants before their departure from the village determines what they do and where they go outside the village and agriculture. Members of the land-owning classes tend to leave the village equipped with education and capital. They try to establish a foothold in the formal sector of the economy, go abroad as contract workers to countries in West Asia or may even settle as Non-Resident Indians (NRIs) in East Africa, North America, Europe and Australia. In such cases, migration is a manifestation of globalisation.

For others, horizontal or geographical mobility does not mean vertical or economic mobility; the fact that they migrate does not substantially better their condition. For them, migration does not end misery; migration may, at best, merely diminish poverty.

Our focus is on those who make up the large underclass of land-poor and landless workers stuck at the bottom of the rural order. They go out to sell their labour power and come back after short or long periods of absence. Their work migration is in the nature of circulation of wage labour, resulting in low rates of savings or none at all. Nevertheless, the village and its people are on the move.

Babubhai, an adivasi, ran away from home when 10 years old to work in Bombay for 18 years. A row with his *seth* and the realisation that he had not made any real progress, not even enough to support his wife and children, made him return to his landless hamlet in Chikhligam near Surat, bitter but secure in familiar surroundings. Tragedy pursued him though, when his somewhat educated teenage son committed suicide for want of a job

4

ON THE MOVE

n the early years of independent India when the national project held out hope for labour too, a very optimistic Hindi film, *Shri 420*, depicted workers on the move. In the very opening sequence of the film, a migrant in search of work sang:

> *Nikal chalein hain khuli sadak par*
>
> *Apnaa seenaa taaney*
>
> *Manzil kaun, kahaan ruknaa hai*
>
> *Ooparwaalaa jaaney*
>
> *Chalnaa jeewan ki kahaani*
>
> *Ruknaa maut ki nishaani*

(With pride in my heart, I have set out on the open road. God alone knows what is my destination and where I have to stop. What I know is that constant mobility is the story of my life and stopping is the sign of death).

While the song did reflect the spirit of the workers who are on the move, it also definitely romanticised the migrant labourers. The fact is that while constant mobility is indeed the lot of many workers, their movement is not random, undirected, or unplanned. Most workers who migrate know where they are headed.

There are of course a few 'floaters'. These are mainly distress and despair migrants who leave their homes because of life-threatening crises like drought, floods, communal riots, etc. There are also some vagrants, homeless and destitute, living out life as beggars and mendicants. Such migrants — including the very young and the very old — may go wherever life takes them.

However, most workers who take to the roads have a fairly clear idea of their destination. They set out to sell their labour and the few petty commodities they can trade in and, by and large, they are aware of the markets for these. The channels of information available to such workers may not have the elaborateness of sophisticated Management Information Systems (MIS) but they do serve to convey relevant knowledge. Labour contractors, *mukadams* or jobbers, gang leaders, other workers who have gone out and returned, friends, people from the same caste, particularly relatives — all these  constitute sources of information about the demand for labour and possibilities of finding specific kinds of work. Indeed the *mukadam* in some respects acts as a traffic policeman, regulating the flow of labour in specific directions as well as imposing penalties.

Armed with such knowledge about the market and carrying whatever tools they can gather, the workers set out. Some head for places where they believe unskilled labour is in demand: on road construction or urban building sites or stone quarries, places where spades, shovels and pick-axes are the most prominent tools of the trade.

Others go to towns, entering with apprehension writ large on their faces. Yet others carry to the bustle of the cities their headloads of tradeable goods, mostly perishable commodities like vegetables, which have to be sold that very day. All of them work in the informal sector of the economy on the basis of the informal channels of communication regarding the market for labour and various goods.

Such information is useful not only for workers but it also helps employers. It is important for them to have some idea of the 'source of labour'; hence jobbers are vital in the process of migration for work. Indeed, in many cases, even the transportation of labour by tractors or trucks is organised by jobbers who perform a vital intermediary function. Just as workers need recommendations, employers too need references regarding the 'reliability' of the labourers who need to be 'spoken for'. This is particularly important for jobs which require

▶ **All available hands, even those of children, are required for cutting cane. The 'hands' — and the accompanying bodies — are carted off to the fields, escorted by the employer on his gleaming motorcycle**

some skills and are of a relatively longer duration. Jobbers provide the necessary mediation since employers also want to keep their distance from the workers who are not local but are mere migrants with whom no long-term relationship need be established.

Of course, migrants seeking work are of different types. There are those who leave their abode in the morning but return at the end of the day or night. Many casual workers, or itinerant vendors of petty merchandise — vegetables, fruits, eggs, twigs for cleaning teeth, and other similar items — are daily migrants of this type. They travel to nearby hamlets or town to peddle their wares or to sell their labour.

Most of them travel by foot, only being able to cover the area that is within walking distance. However, there are others whose range of income-seeking is extended because they own bicycles. Some even commute daily by train to big cities.

◀ **The twigs that serve as toothbrushes are cut from trees in the village and in the forest and brought daily for sale to the towns and cities. The twig-seller spends a considerable part of her earnings on transport since she has to travel long distances by train as the forests recede from the cities**

Other migrants leave their villages for longer periods, carrying their worldly goods with them wherever they go. There is a certain seasonality to their movements: they leave their villages when there is little work, go to other rural work sites like brick kilns or quarries or to towns and cities but return to their villages when agricultural operations require their presence. Such circulation of labour also creates an organic linkage between different sectors of the economy.

▼ **If economics is the study of 'man's workday goods', it should be easy enough to account for the pathetic possessions of these migrant workers**

There are yet other workers who leave their homes and travel long distances, in quite a large number of cases right across the country, to find work in mills, sheds and other urban enterprises. They live in the city for months, sometimes years, returning to their villages occasionally, for rest and recuperation as it

were, but most of their working life is spent as unsettled migrants, rootless in their place of work.

Many workers — especially those who find work in the agricultural sector or are engaged in non-agricultural but rural jobs — often take to the road in family groups. Men, women and children go together, setting up camp wherever they can find work. Sometimes these camps are obviously temporary, just a makeshift clearing in a field, with their pathetic bundles of worldly goods arrayed around them. Sometimes, itinerant

The selling of labour — on a casual, daily basis — is not easy. Like other marketable commodities, labour too must be displayed. And the city centre is often the best place for such display

artisans set up their workstations wherever they can find place to live, even forging metal on pavements, selling what they can and moving on to another site. Sometimes, the shelter is in the shadow of the city, transient arrangements which over time congeal into slums whose residents service those who live in high-rise apartment buildings.

Work-related migration is both rural–urban and rural–rural, and the mode of travel depends

on the distance covered as well as the period of absence. If there is daily commuting, there is no need to shift 'home' but even if the migration is for a couple of weeks, the migrant has to create a habitat: it may be a temporary shelter under trees by the roadside or a wretched, ramshackle hut run up out of sticks, rotting planks, dirty rags and even cardboard. Even the use of bricks to build temporary shelters at construction sites does not disguise the ephemeral nature of the migrant workers' presence there: once the work gets over, the worker goes away.

The most dramatic evidence in the towns and cities of the worker

organisations of workers go hand in hand with mass unemployment and casualisation of labour. All this has, in many respects, reversed the processes of production itself — from being carried out in factories to once again being fragmented into manufactories. The consequences are severe for the labour process as well as for the labouring people.

This book seeks to portray the life and labour of precisely such workers.

▼ **Under the clock tower, near the bus station, in the *chowk*, 'manpower' waits from early in the morning to be hired for the job or the day**

as a migrant, as a 'casual', as a member of the amorphous informal sector, is the sight of work-seekers gathered in the mornings at specific places: under the town's clock tower, at cross-roads, near railway stations, at bus stands, at the entry point of cities, along markets. There they wait to be engaged to sell their skills, their strength, their raw labour power. Those among them who have some skills are a little more confident. Those who have their own tools are a little more dignified. But, in the end, they are all mere commodities — to be haggled over, 'purchased' for the day or for the job and taken away to the work site. The presence of trade unions and other

5

WORK SITES & PROCESSES

The very mention of the term 'work sites' in the context of labour conjures up pictures of factories with assembly lines, pictures made immortal by the only slight exaggeration by Charlie Chaplin in *Modern Times*. However, while that picture is to some extent true even in these 'post-modern, post-industrial times', it is not correct with regard to labour in the informal sector. The work sites of such labour are not well-organised factories absorbing a large, massed workforce; they are a variety of places, as varied as the very processes of work, and occupied by small groups of men, women and children.

The work sites of labour in the informal sector can be in cramped manufactories, within households, in slums, or even under the open skies on streets, quarries, riverbeds and banks and fields. These 'natural' locations of work often pit the worker against nature itself and often succeed in dwarfing man in the environment where he labours for a living.

Indeed, many such workers toil in the open air where their labour should be visible to all; and yet a certain cover seems to hang over their work sites making them and their abysmal conditions of work practically invisible. These are so easily taken for granted that the stone quarries, the brick kilns, even the forges and foundries they set up on urban streets are not noticed even if they are seen. Among those who, seen and unseen, operate in the streets are

▼ **Itinerant tinkers forging brass idols on the streetside using the simplest of methods and the crudest of tools**

hawkers and vendors, beggars and rag-pickers, caterers and entertainers, artisans and craftsmen, tinkers and repairers, and of course, the transport workers: road-builders, cart-pullers, headload carriers. The characteristic features of their work environment are milling crowds, pollution, dust, dirt and deafening noise.

An important aspect of such work is also the need to cope with the weather. Work must go on day and night and the open-air informal sector

▶ **Cobblers, craftsmen and food vendors vie for whatever space they can squeeze out for themselves on crowded pavements**

must devise methods to meet the challenges of nature whether it is the blistering heat of summer, the pouring rain of the monsoon or the chilling winds of winter. The weather as a factor of production has not been taken note of but it does play a significant role in day-to-day work as well as in imposing on work the cycles of seasonality.

Of course, seasonality of work is not specific to open-air workers. Many of those who work indoors also encounter seasonality in the market

▶ **In the open, work tends to get interrupted by the weather, be it rain, heat or cold**

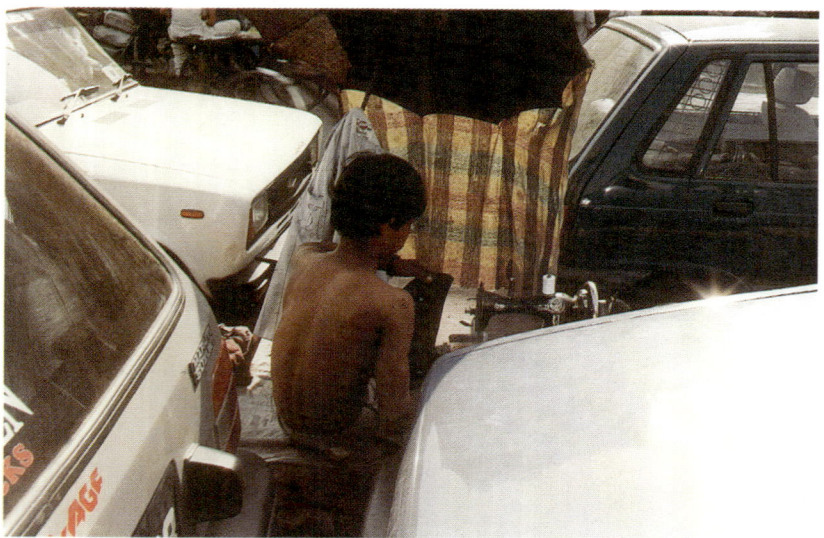

for their labour. This may have to do with the availability of raw materials or with the variable demand for their products but the result, as far as workers are concerned, is that they are not assured of employment or wages through the year. This too contributes to the informal sector worker being transitory, mobile, unsettled.

Both indoors and outdoors, whatever be the site of work, labourers engage in work organised under different contracts. They may take up

▶ **Preparing thread for the kite-flying festival. Seasonality of work is a common feature for informal sector workers, with some activities lasting just a few days**

employment as single individuals, as headload carriers for instance, or they might be hired as gang labour on construction sites or on road repair works. They might also work in family based units, inside homes as in the many branches of the textile industry, or even in the brick kilns where adults, children and even infants all work and live together. In some cases, as among the households engaged in brocade and embroidery for the market, the familial nature of the work organisation disguises its waged character: what appears to be self-employment is only the family earning wages collectively by taking in work as available. The myth of 'respectable' self-activity, even with a 'middle-class' veneer, is maintained to distinguish such workers who work in their own abode and are 'local' from those who are obviously recent and still unsettled migrants into the city.

In the Surat region of western India, these latter workers arrive from various parts of Gujarat and from other distant states of India. They group themselves according to ethnicity, caste and even on the basis of special skills and also get employed in such groups. Thus there are tribal road-builders from the Panch Mahals; construction workers from Rajasthan; 'Malibhais' from Orissa and 'Bhaiyas' from Uttar Pradesh as powerloom workers; Patels from Saurashtra who work as diamond cutters and polishers, Malayalam speakers from Kerala toiling in the repair shops along the highways; 'Khandeshis' from Maharashtra migrating annually to harvest the sugarcane.

The organisation of labour according to regional, linguistic, ethnic and caste groupings underscores the stereotypes about such workers. For instance, among the first workers to have come from Orissa to

▶ **The usage of *coolie*, a word that belonged to colonial jargon implying hard physical labour, has been forbidden by government regulation because of its derogatory meaning. But informal sector workers continue to be dealt with as *coolies***

▲ **Workers at a diamond atelier are watched hawkeyed by ever-present supervisors**

Surat in search of employment, a few got jobs as gardeners and were therefore labelled 'Malibhais'. Subsequently, thousands, even hundreds of thousands of Orissan workers have migrated to Surat to work on its powerlooms but the 'Malibhai' name sticks to the whole community. 'Bhaiya' too, used for Hindi-speaking migrants from Uttar Pradesh and Bihar, is ambiguous; literally it means 'brother' but it carries an undertone of disrespect for one so addressed and presumed to be rustic, illiterate and rough.

The ethnic stereotypes also broadly correspond to a simple labour division: the many forms of production in the informal sector take place in a 'flat landscape' which might have a low level of complexity — often with crude exploitation of raw unskilled labour — but in most cases with a high degree of surveillance. It is not only in the diamond polishing workshops that the worker is under constant watch; even when the raw material is merely the earth, as in the brick kilns, the employer or the supervisor is ever-present, keeping an eye on every move of the worker, now scolding, now cajoling, now abusing, ensuring that the maximum amount of labour is extracted.

The labour intensity of work in the informal sector does not require or allow for complexity in the division of work. Operations are, by and large, simple and not based on a high level of

▶ **The body language of the *seth* says it all — his workers need to be disciplined by mouth and hand, sometimes also by physical violence**

skills. There are, of course, some specialised activities, which call for particular types of labour from specific regions with special skills, but generally the division of work is simple enough. It is based on age and gender: women are helpers and remain so throughout their working lives and men are the only 'skilled' workers. There is a significant need to contextualise child workers in the informal sector. They are present in almost all activities; in many cases they do not even receive wages but provide a much-needed labour input, which is calculated as part of the output of the adults.

In addition to the blatant exploitation of labour, what characterises the informal sector is the crude technology, low capital investment, the excessively manual nature of production within it. At the same time, the sector is also marked by high rates of profit and enormous capital accumulation assisted by the fact that the informal sector is, by definition, not registered, let alone taxed. One of the most telling pictures of this sector is the sight of the 'gentlemanly' owner of a garbage shop, sitting in his well-ironed clothes by his gleaming motorcycle, amidst the piles of waste that the rag-pickers have painfully sorted out for him to profit from.

Rags to riches, indeed!

▶ **Rag-picking and scavenging all kinds of waste — in this case just outside the massive walls of the Surat fort — is often women's work**

THE WEFT AND THE WARP

The fame of Surat as a prime centre of textile production predates the colonial era. However, the character of its textile industry took a new turn in the middle of the twentieth century when handlooms fell into disuse as they were replaced by powerlooms. By the beginning of the 1980s there were 105,000 authorised and unauthorised powerlooms, about half the total capacity in the entire country at that time, installed in sheds called *galas*. It has been estimated that, in 1992–3, at least 250,000 powerlooms were in operation and that number has since grown to 400,000.

The phenomenal development of this industry in Surat was directly related to the dismantling of textile mills in Mumbai and Ahmedabad during the same period. Mill-owners in those traditional centres of the textile industry complained about what they described as the excessive cost of labour, a consequence of strong trade unionisation in the formal sector of the economy, and used this argument to refuse to make new investments. Consequently, the cotton textile industry got 'sick' and mill after mill closed down. The closure of these mills explains the remarkable fact that in the 1970s no less than 70 per cent of the

▶ **The labour-intensive transport of the grey cloth to and from the textile market is handled by a huge army of cart-pullers and headloaders paid on a piece-rate basis for each load they carry and each run they make. They are, of course, not paid for the time they have to hang around waiting for new orders**

powerlooms operating in Surat were second-hand!

The powerloom sector is notable for the small-scale nature of its enterprises. By the middle of the 1980s, roughly half of the *galas* were still equipped with less than 10 looms each. The owners were almost all Gujaratis, most of them original inhabitants of Surat. Indeed, many of them started operating their businesses from their homes, with the entire family — men, women and children — all engaged in the enterprise.

Nowadays the majority of *galas* work on hired labour and the streets of Surat throb day and night with the motion of its powerlooms on which workers toil. And yet, the total amount paid in wages in this highly labour-intensive industry has been estimated to represent a minor part of all costs of production, not more than 10 to 11 per cent of the sale value of 'grey' or unprocessed fabric. Fibre and other basic materials represent three-quarters of all production costs.

of the industry in India's principal artificial silk — or 'art silk' — centre was further articulated by the transfer to Surat of the wholesale trade in semi-finished and finished textile products. A number of huge skyscrapers were built in which traders and producers or their agents bargain for terms and conditions. It is estimated that at present there are over 20 textile markets in this area housing 3,000 shops.

Until the mid-1970s, the larger part of the woven product was sold to factories outside Gujarat for further processing. This loss of 'value-addition' was stopped, however, when more and more dyeing and printing mills were set up in Surat. Around 1960, forty such units were operating in the city, which together employed not more than 500 workers. The workforce has since increased to at least 40,000 — almost exclusively male — spread over several hundreds of dyeing units. In later years, the progressive trend towards vertical integration

The earlier mode of production of artificial silk firms, i.e. domestic manufacture by owners who depended primarily on family labour, was retained for a longer period in the brocade industry. Surat has always been the centre for this century-old *jari* handwork, i.e. the application of gold and silver thread to fine textiles, which used to be the monopoly of a few local artisanal castes with a working tradition that dated as far back as the time of the Mughals. In the past, the limited clientele for this luxury product came from the highest echelons of the population. This situation has changed due to the growing prosperity of the middle classes. At the same time, the reduced quality of the materials used — copper and artificial silk instead of the much more expensive gold and silver thread — has broadened the market for *jari*-worked textiles. *Saris* in which precious metal thread is used — and of which the most expensive may cost some tens of thousands of rupees — now form an essential part of the wedding trousseau for the relatively well to do.

◀ **A house-based worker doing intricate embroidery work on art silk fabric**

Surat, with 80 per cent of the total annual brocade production in the country, has managed to retain its position as the principal place of manufacture of *jari* to cater to the strongly increased national and foreign demand for the commodity. Towards the end of the 1980s, brocade and embroidery firms in the city provided work for 30,000–35,000 people, of whom 70 per cent were women. The combined labour force in smaller centres elsewhere in south

▼ **Handling yarn at home. Both the very young and the old are roped in for gainful work**

Gujarat is almost as large. Small producers who manufacture the metal thread and apply it to textile, working at home and using their own tools, are known as *akhadedars*. If the labour power provided by the household — including women and children — is insufficient, they employ outside workers. Among the women and girls employed in this branch of industry, 81 per cent are no longer unpaid family labour but nowadays work for wages. Some of them are taken on as extra workers in the homes of small producers, but many more are employed by big owners who have transferred production to separate workshops employing 10–60 labourers. Surprisingly, however, the increasing conversion of self-employed home-workers into wage-labourers has not been accompanied by any change in the social identity of the workforce.

As in the *jari* industry, the first generation of workers in the artificial silk industry also came from Surat's own population. The most recent — 1962 — issue of the Surat District Gazetteer dryly notes their dominance in the industry at the end of the 1950s: 'Khatris, Mohamedans, Harijans and other backward class people were engaged in this industry. Most of the labourers were illiterate and spendthrift.'

The enormous expansion in this industry since then has been coupled with the substitution of migrants for local workers. Any estimate of the total workforce can only be guesswork. The degree of under-registration in official industrial statistics makes all official data simply worthless. An estimate of 215,000 workers in the art silk industry (170,000 in powerloom workshops, 45,000 in dyeing and printing mills), i.e. nearly one out of four wage workers in the city, seemed not to be an unduly high figure in the beginning of the 1990s.

▼ **Children employed to do home-based *jari* work. Their nimble fingers are an asset in this type of intricate work**

The workforce is predominantly male, more than half in the 15–25 age group. Only one in ten powerloom operators is older than forty. The labour process is so exhausting that very few are able to perform adequately after middle age. Once the ability to maintain production drops below the required level, older workers are discharged without mercy. There is no shortage of young people willing to take their place.

Women and children are also present in the workshops, in roughly equal proportion, and together represent 12–15 per cent of the workforce employed in the powerloom sector. They are usually involved in the various preparatory processes that synthetic thread has to undergo (winding, twisting, beam passing) before weaving can commence.

Working and living conditions are wretched. The workers derive no security at all from their employment. Only a quarter of them are listed in their employer's administration under their true names. They are paid on a piece-work basis, and their monthly income is dependent

◄ **Workers in the folding and packing department of a dyeing-and-printing mill. There are about 300 such units which produce mainly *saris* for the growing middle-class market**

on the degree of self-exploitation that they achieve during a 12-hour day or night shift. Women workers are paid less than the men are. They are all debarred from allowances and fringe benefits that secure the lives of workers in the formal sector. An indication of the lonely life the migrant workers lead in the city is that 85 per cent of the more than 200,000 Oriya labourers at work in the textile industry in 1992 stayed in Surat without spouse or parents. As single migrants, the majority of married men are separated from wives and children who stay in the villages and to whom they send a maximal part of earnings whenever possible.

Surat's textile workers can be classified at best as semi-permanent. Their employers do not even record the most elementary personal particulars about the workers in their business records. This situation came to light tragically in the summer of 1981 when an illegally constructed dyeing-and-printing mill collapsed just as the day and night shifts were being changed. Most of the 1,200 workers were fortunately pulled out alive from the wreckage. The lack of official record, however, prevented many of the dead from being identified.

A quarter of all workers in the artificial silk industry move to a different factory within a year. The analysis of work profiles shows that in most cases a change is made more than once and that it is not restricted to the initial period after arriving in the city. In such circumstances, links with the place of employment cannot be other than extremely tenuous, as a research report notes: 'There is such a rapid turnover of workers, especially over small weaving units, that in several cases the respondents are not sufficiently familiar with their current workplaces to provide details like the number and background of other persons employed in the workplaces for various operations in different shifts. Even some veteran workers were unable to remember the total number of different units they had worked in during their careers and perhaps no amount of probing could have helped in such cases.'

The reasons given for high mobility are the prospects of higher wages or bad relations with the former employer. But these arguments incorrectly suggest that it is the employee who takes the decision to leave. In fact, a worker is frequently dismissed for very diverse reasons: fall in production; his or her absence due to illness; disinclination on part of the employer to grant leave; or displacement of the older worn-out workers in favour of recommended newcomers.

The notion that rural migrants refuse to fully commit themselves to industrial work and life because they stubbornly prefer to keep one foot in the village and the other in agriculture has remained a recurrent explanation in the literature on the high rate of turnover in urban employment. Reports sponsored by Surat employers' associations suggest a similar tendency among the footloose proletariat employed in textile production.

This interpretation overlooks the possibility that the murderous work pace leaves the migrants no option but to go home from time to time in order to recuperate. Another reason is that the uneven rhythm of production over the year makes it attractive for the employer to lay off part of the workforce during the slack period and, conversely, to recruit more hands when demand picks up again. Indeed, urban employment in the informal sector is marked by a seasonal cyclicality that is usually only associated with an agrarian-rural economic lifestyle. Employers refuse to guarantee that workers who absent themselves or are sent off will be taken back on their return. The industrialist is motivated by a single interest: to keep the looms in operation day and night and for as many days per year as possible. That ambition has priority over maintenance of labour relations based on stability. Given the abundant

▶ **What looks like a single factory is split up into different work units. Separate labour gangs operate under their own sub-contractors and have no relationship at all with the owner of the factory premises**

labour supply, employers determine conditions of work as well as wages.

The workers who serve the powerlooms in Surat lack all those restrictive and protective conditions that make employment in the formalised sector of the economy attractive. The long hours of work in the weaving units go back to the time when this industry was still run as a family business and under the monopoly of local craftsmen. All members of the household used to participate in the production process, which went on in an uneven rhythm all hours of the day and night.

The work regime has since become more capitalistic. The workers do not belong to the family or even the same caste anymore and the intimate relationship between capital and labour that earlier existed has clearly ceased. The loom operators are hired hands only who, however, have not been given the type of protection enjoyed by the workforce in the formal sector of the economy. Although the Factory Act expressly stipulates a working day of no more than eight hours, almost all employers give their weavers no other choice than to stand behind the machines for twelve hours at a stretch.

That these conditions prevail in the powerloom sheds of other cities like Surat is illustrated in a report on the same industry in Ichalkaranji, a town in Maharashtra: '"The twelve-hour shift is a real bitch. Gnaws at our lives it does!" ... "Twelve-hour shift? Not eight?" ... "Oh no! 8-8 full twelve hours. And you can't go off like in other factories because all pay is by piecework. 13 paise per metre. We have to keep the loom going till the other shift arrives. Then we put our mark on the cloth and get up." Another, a little older, said, "That twelve-hour shift kills a man. By the time we get home after the shift we are like zombies. Some get drunk on the way home; some not. Put some junk in the tummy and go out like a light. Get up and come to work."'

And if a member of the next shift does not turn up to take their place, then the workers have to continue operating the looms until they are relieved 24 hours later. Such an extreme lengthening of work time is not disagreeable to the powerloom operator. In line with the law of self-exploitation, he makes use of each and every opportunity to maximise his income. This is naturally impossible without one or two brief intervals, but it is typical of the industrial climate in the informal sector where most workshops have no formal rules regarding intervals. The weaver who rests a little, eats something, or has to go to the toilet, remains accountable for anything that might go wrong during his short absence.

Shortage of electrical power makes it unavoidable that workplaces in Surat close down for one day each week. That is the only reason, caused by the interrupted use of capital, that the workers are given a day off. In fact they are not paid on the day that the looms have to close down. This also applies when workers take any leave, which they have to do on their own account and at their own risk. A weaver is fortunate if, on his return, he does not find that his place has been taken by another.

Piece-work is generally the customary method of payment of labour throughout all layers of the informal sector. It also applies to the power-looms. Weavers are paid per metre of woven material, and management bases itself on an average daily production per machine. The amount is based on what a hard and skilled worker can produce in 12 hours. If the output of a newcomer or an older hand remains below that norm, not incidentally but systematically, then he is discharged by his employer who thus puts an end to the under-utilisation of his capital investment.

The new workplaces occupied by powerlooms are relatively large, but the people working among the machines have hardly space in which to move around. The enormous noise of the looms and the heat under the corrugated zinc roof are sources of discomfort. The callousness of the industry is revealed by the tone of a report sponsored by the employers' association. Regarding the appalling work conditions to which the industrial proletariat is exposed, the report notes: '...largely due to insanitary living conditions, the health of the workers is affected and absenteeism from work is noticed. It is difficult to attribute all health problems to the working conditions or long hours of working as most diseases are not work-related. Diseases like chronic headaches, stomach problems and skin infections could hardly be work-related. These are more likely to be due to lack of nutritious diet and maybe, to drinking habits. For hearing problems or deafness in the weaving industry, there is no solution. It is, however, true that if safety precautions are observed, problems like electrical shocks, chemical burns, physical injuries due to fall, etc., could be prevented. It is sad to note that, in the majority of factories, even first aid facilities are not provided.'

In fact, noise is the greatest evil as far as the powerloom workers are concerned. Even when the streets are quiet at night, the continual

▶ **These looms were earlier installed in mills. After the closure of the mills, the looms were sold and came to life again in the powerloom workshops**

rattle of the machines in buildings echoes in many parts of the town. Investigations into conditions in this industry showed that 78 per cent of the respondents suffered from fairly serious health complaints, particularly hearing disorders, eye diseases, bronchial complaints and chronic pain in the head or limbs.

Even worse than the situation of weavers is that of workers in the dyeing-and-printing mills who have to handle dyes often with their bare hands and inhale the noxious smells of chemicals. And then there are those who, in a closed space with very high humidity, operate a machine with a high piercing sound, which treats artificial silk yarn in such a way that the threads are loosened and curled. However, both statistics and research on work hazards, industrial injuries and occupational diseases that disproportionately afflict people in the informal sector, are sadly lacking.

The industrial townships on the edge of Surat, in particular Udhana and Pandesara, are bad places in which to stay, let alone in which to work. Environmental pollution, of air and water, is unimaginable. Dense smoke, soot and dust make it difficult to breathe, and even a brief foray into this jungle of modern industry leaves the eyes burning and nose running. The same applies to industrial sites in other places along the highway and the railroad, which form the connections with Mumbai in the south and Vadodara/Ahmedabad in the north. Farmers in the south Gujarat western coastal plain complain about the damage to their crops and land caused by the effluents from the chemical industry that has been set up here. Employment in any of these industries entails a considerable health risk, as labourers have experienced. They have to handle corrosive salts and acids without any protection at all for face, arms and legs.

'I can show you the wounds on my hands,' said a worker, 'but not the pain that I feel inside my body.'

◀ **Due to the handling of chemical dyes with their bare hands, and the constant exposure to their fumes in the dyeing-and-printing units, these labourers have a short work stint as well as life span**

BEHIND THE GLITTER

The history of diamond cutting and polishing in Surat illustrates the way in which local workers have been superseded by migrants from other districts. In the mid-1950s the city had slightly more than 100 ateliers employing barely 500 workers. By the end of the 1960s these had already increased to more than 1,000 cutting and polishing establishments with 20,000 workers. Persistent drought from 1966–8 drove thousands of young Kanbi Patels, belonging to the locally dominant peasant caste, out of the villages around Bhavnagar in Saurashtra to the diamond ateliers in south Gujarat at the opposite end of the Gulf of Cambay.

The school-going boys abandoned their studies and came to Surat and Navsari in search of jobs in this field. These youths were apprenticed for three years on very meagre wages — only the cost of their food was met by the employers.

Once the connection was made, the expansion continued and

▲ **As an ancient port of great fame Surat has been a centre for the production of wealth and splendour. Today diamonds have become a global commodity. They are imported as raw stones and exported cut and polished, i.e. with value added by labour**

even accelerated in the next decade. In 1978–9, there were almost 5,700 workplaces with a registered workforce of 41,000. Punctuated by short-term recessions, the increase has continued. In 1982, it was estimated that there were over 9,000 units with workers totalling 57,500. According to official statistics, unit size throughout this period remained very modest, averaging six or seven workers.

The explosive growth in the number of units

▼ Much of the money in the diamond industry is part of the cash circulation which goes unaccounted in government records and is thus not taxed for the public good either

was caused by the fairly small amount of cash needed as starting capital. Wages formed no less than 86 per cent of all production expenses. Good relations with traders are a more important precondition for setting up an enterprise than the availability of cash money. This also explains why the majority of new owners are former cutters. The workers, *hiravalas*, are mostly young persons in the 18–25 age bracket and, at the same time, only 2 per cent of entrepreneurs have inherited their business from an earlier generation.

These impressive growth figures only approximate the actual situation, however, and need to be adjusted upwards. Research based on sample surveys has shown that government registration leaves a great deal to be desired. There are more diamond cutting firms in Surat than is officially known. The number of workers is also much higher than the stated average of six or seven per unit. Taking these factors into account, it is estimated that there was a total of around 90,000 workers in the industry at the beginning of the 1990s, a number which makes it clear why Surat is called the Diamond City of India. Of late, production has expanded to other centres, such as Ahmedabad.

Even an average of ten to twelve workers per workshop makes no real difference to the small-scale nature of production. Ateliers are situated mostly in the densely populated city centre, in accommodation that is so small that association with sweatshops easily springs to mind. Women are conspicuous by their absence, unlike in Thrissur, a town in southern India where the industry was introduced more recently and where the employment of women has become quite routine.

About half the diamond cutters in Surat city live in one-person households, indicating their bachelor status. They may rent accommodation singly, but usually do so in small groups. It is a type of lifestyle to which slightly skilled and relatively better paid migrant workers, who form the majority of the workforce, are also accustomed.

Less than one-third of the workers were born and grew up in Surat. More than half of all diamond cutters at work in the city come from far away, from Saurashtra or the north of Gujarat, and nearly all are Kanbi Patels, originally a peasant caste. This contrasts strongly with the situation at the inception of the industry, when the workforce consisted solely of inhabitants of Surat. Those locals were soon joined by migrants from the direct vicinity of the city and they in turn were forced

▶ **The cut and polished stones are sold in the open streets by an infinite number of tradesmen or their agents, each with their breastpockets loaded with pouches of diamonds**

into a minority position by immigrants from further afield. Two regions — the Saurashtra area and Mehsana and Palanpur districts — have been the major contributors to the more recent influx, accounting for about 70 per cent of the migrant workforce.

During the second half of the 1970s more and more diamond ateliers were opened in the direct hinterland of Surat. Navsari emerged as a secondary nucleus for the industry, while units varying in number from a few dozen to some hundreds were set up in most principal towns of the sub-districts in south Gujarat. During the first phase, the initiative for this expansion was taken mostly by cutters who had gained some expertise in well-established urban workshops and, with support from traders, took the risk of starting up for themselves in small towns close to their home villages. Many were sons of Kanbi Patidaris, members of a dominant peasant caste in rural south Gujarat. At first they recruited workers from their own milieu. Tribals came later, and even they were mostly limited to members of land-owning households. Halpatis were only considered in years of explosive growth, when atelier owners were prepared to train people as cutters whom they would have refused in normal times. Close to their own rural milieu, the inclusion of Halpatis is rather less exceptional than in Surat city. Their share in the total workforce in this labour-intensive industry, however, is extremely small, and they were the first to be discharged when a major slump occurred in the late 1980s.

By that time the diamond industry of Surat started to lose some of its former buoyancy. Competition and recession both resulted in a cutback in the number of jobs, which had gone up to more than one hundred thousand a few years earlier, by some tens of thousands.

▼ **A young boy in his teens trains as an apprentice, carrying out a tedious trade for which he is paid very little or no wage at all**

Many Kanbi Patel boys who had been trained in Surat as diamond cutters went back home to Bhavnagar to set up their own workshops. In addition to this shift away from the capital of the diamond industry in Gujarat, the international economic slump also caused a temporary fall in demand for this costly product, whether for industrial purposes or for jewellery. Probably far more significant in the somewhat longer term is the increasing competition by new centres of production elsewhere in the world, particularly China, North Korea and Vietnam. The immediate result is that the number of diamond workers in Surat and other places in south Gujarat has fallen during the last few years.

To be taken as a diamond cutter in Surat is just an initial step in an occupational career that continues to be characterised by very high mobility. This applies in particular to those who were not born and bred in Surat. At least one-third of the diamond cutters who have come to the city from elsewhere report having changed their job within the space of a year. After the second year this increases to almost 50 per cent. The reasons why diamond cutters change so frequently from one employer to another are the prospect of a somewhat higher wage and the wish for a more compatible work atmosphere. Another consideration may be lack of sufficient work or closure of the business.

The ready availability of jobs, especially for those known to be highly skilled, only partly explains this frequent job shifting. Workers expect to be treated well and may quit their jobs if bossed over. Some workers have an exaggerated notion of their skill and expect to be advanced substantial loans due to highly skilled workers. When these hopes do not materialise, they try to save face by quitting. The ability of a *karkhanedar* (factory owner) to retain his workers also depends on whether he

▼ **Diamond cutters are forced to leave the tiffin carriers in which they bring their food outside the wretched buildings in which ateliers are set up**

has enough contacts with merchants to obtain a steady supply of good quality raw diamonds. If he is unable to retain a steady supply, or if the diamonds are of poor quality and difficult to work on, the workers may look for jobs elsewhere.

This may suggest that the initiative towards breaking off the relationship is taken by the employee who apparently has considerable latitude. Such a situation can indeed be found, but only when the worker is known to be an excellent craftsman and, moreover, comes from a similar social milieu as his employer. This applies particularly when both employer and employee are Kanbi Patels. In such cases, the cutter may consider himself the equal of his patron and in fact intends eventually to set up shop himself.

In contrast, diamond cutters who belong to the low castes of landless labourers are less assertive. When they leave their jobs it is for quite different reasons. A survey of diamond workers in Surat notes, 'Workers from such a background are submissive to their employer and rarely talk back. They blindly carry out the jobs assigned to them and

are apt to harbour animosities rather than give them free vent. As a consequence, animosities sometimes build up to such a level that it becomes impossible for the worker to continue in his job.'

However, compared to workers in other parts of the informal sector, the diamond cutters have a relatively better life. This is also expressed in the greater latitude they are given in performing their daily tasks. A survey of their life and work conditions notes: 'Diamond workers start and stop at their convenience. Workers who stay in the town may commence work as early as 7 a.m. Those who stay in the surrounding villages commute to work by cycle, bus or train. Buses and trains are not noted for their punctuality and travelling by cycle is problematic during the monsoon months. These workers report for work by nine or even ten o'clock in the morning. Workers also have their lunch break or noon rest at a time convenient to them. By five o'clock in the evening workers begin to leave, but some may continue working up to seven or eight o'clock in the evening.'

At first sight, this relaxed manner of employment, certainly as regards its flexibility, compares favourably even with the more comfortable working conditions in some segments of the formal sector economy. Piece-work payment plays an important role, however. It sometimes leads to this type of more skilled labour taking an attitude that can be associated with the work mentality of the petite bourgeoisie. Diamond cutters are paid per stone. The work tempo that they maintain — to come to work or not, to start and finish earlier or later, to work harder or more slowly — determines the amount of their earnings. If the work does not go right, if a stone is difficult to cut, the worker may decide to let go for the day. The survey notes about the diamond cutter, 'He may quit work early to watch a movie or roam about the market place. In the matter of leave too there are few restrictions on the workers. While some are considerate enough to inform the *karkhanedar* in advance, others fail to do so. In the agricultural harvesting season some workers who come from villages absent themselves to engage in harvesting. They say that this arrangement works out to their advantage financially. On the whole, the workers do not like a lean pay packet, and this is what keeps them on the job 6 days a week.'

This last remark is not in the least superfluous, even if only to avoid the impression that diamond workers form the sort of 'labour aristocracy' that can be found in the formal sector of the economy. The owner of the workplace accepts such behaviour only from his best workers whom he does not want to lose. The others not only work long hours if the patron so wishes, but are also given little latitude to regulate their own presence or absence.

In most branches of industry, the labour

process has such a degrading effect that, for that reason alone, employers feel forced regularly to replace and replenish their workforce. This is, however, less applicable to diamond workshops. The term 'sweatshop' perfectly illustrates the immediate and principal impression gained from visits to these establishments in Surat, Navsari and Bardoli as also of the workshops where gold jewellery is fashioned by immigrant Bengali craftsmen who produce the most intricate items for the export market.

In a small room with no ventilation, lit with neon tubes but without fresh air, ten or more young men sit cross-legged and close together on the floor around *ghantis*, work benches, closely watched by the owner from his air-conditioned cubicle. A towel hanging around the worker's neck is used to dry hands and face of the sweat that runs profusely, particularly in the summer heat. The boss does not allow any fresh air into the atelier out of fear that his workers might rob him of diamonds by throwing some of the valuable stones given to them for processing out of the window or use any other opening to the outside world for that purpose. It is in these degrading circumstances that the dazzling diamond jewels are produced.

▼ **Gold jewellery being crafted by one of the many craftsmen in this trade who have come from Bengal**

CRUSHING CANE AND LABOUR

Huge armies of labour sweep through the Gujarat countryside every year, clearly attuned to the rhythm of the seasons. These are harvest workers who trek through the central plain each year, to cut sugarcane in the fields. An initial study, started in 1977, into their coming and mode of employment throughout the campaign, showed that the majority of the 50,000 men, women and children had been recruited from the neighbouring state of Maharashtra. Ten years later, a repeat survey showed that the army of workers had doubled in the meantime. Since then, the acreage of south Gujarat that is planted with sugarcane has continued to grow. At the end of the 1980s, it could be stated with reasonable certainty that seasonal migrants mobilised for the sugarcane harvest in south Gujarat totalled 150,000. Today their numbers are even greater.

Around the middle of this century, farmers belonging to the dominant Patidar caste in the Bardoli region took the initiative to set up a co-operative sugar mill. This laid the basis for an agro-industrial development that has contributed greatly to the growing prosperity of the large landowners. Most *taluka* towns in south Gujarat now have

their own sugar co-operative, set up for the purpose and owned by farmer-members who have bought one or more shares which give them the right to deliver cane to the mill. The factories operate 24 hours per day, milling the cane brought in from the surrounding areas in quantities ranging from 1,500 to 10,000 tons per day, for six or seven months of the year.

A precondition for such large-scale production was the construction in the 1950s of the Ukai dam on the Tapti river together with a system of irrigation canals that criss-cross the plain. The sugarcane crop that now dominates the local agricultural economy to such an extent is by no means a new commodity. Sugarcane is said to have been one of the most successful cash crops in Bardoli around the mid-nineteenth century and early Survey and Settlement Reports mention its cultivation in other parts of south Gujarat as well. Farmers of that time pressed the cane in their yards in order to make jaggery (*gur*), which was then put into pots and sold to Bombay-based traders. These old sources show that the very labour-intensive cultivation and processing of sugarcane was the main motive why the land-owning village elite employed landless Halpatis all the year round as farm-hands. It was noted around 1930 that '…in the whole of Southern Gujarat, there still obtains a system of labour called the Hali system in which a labourer mortgages his labour to the farmer for a loan he takes for celebrating his marriage. A capitalistic cultivator keeps one or two Halis for performing field operations. He is bound to maintain them whether he exacts work from them or not. He, therefore, deems it wise and profitable to occupy them in sugarcane-cultivation.'

The moral economy of the time more or less obliged landowners to grow certain labour-intensive crops with the explicit intent of guaranteeing local agricultural labourers their basic subsistence. There was a close linkage between sugarcane cultivation and the Hali system, a connection that had continued until Independence and beyond. In those days care for the entire growing cycle, from planting to cane-cutting and transport to the factory, was left entirely to local Halpatis.

Thus the decision by the management of the new farmers' co-operatives to discontinue employing members of the largest landless caste in the region cannot be explained as due to the latter's non-familiarity with this kind of work. Although Halpatis were employed in former times, they have had to make way for outsiders since the modernisation of

crop production in the last few decades. Replacement did not take place gradually but, to some extent, suddenly and completely.

In any case, the impression that until recently by and large agricultural work was by and large done only by local labour is

▼ **Cutting cane still counts as an agricultural operation but should really be understood as a form of industrial production**

◄ Setting out for the fields in the winter cold from the wayside camp. In the summer months, production goes down because of the unbearable heat during the daytime

misleading. Even in the 1960s, and perhaps earlier too, landowners assigned all digging work to Kathiawadis. In the dry season when there is little if anything to do in Saurashtra, these transients came to the villages of south Gujarat in search of work. There were also migrant Halpatis from the more remote hinterland in the district who were hired in gangs by mango-traders to pick fruit that had been bought from growers, often long before the harvest.

It is a fact, however, that some 20 years ago the inflow of migrant labour began to increase strongly. The workers are almost all Adivasi and Dalit (Tribal and Scheduled Caste) peasants from the eastern hills bordering Maharashtra. The need to earn more cash on the one hand and the increasing paucity of land — on account of the increasing pressure of population — particularly due to the felling of forests which had provided many sorts of subsidiary income — on the other hand, have caused an increasing outflow of labour to the plains of south Gujarat. The mass — but nevertheless temporary and cyclical — migration starts immediately after the monsoon. A persistent drought in 1973–4 had accelerated their outflow for part of the year. Acute starvation drove them from their homes, and farmers in south Gujarat found them prepared to work for a whole day for nothing more than a meal.

In 'normal' years these migrant workers come in groups of ten to fifteen men and women around the time for harvesting various crops in order, as they themselves say, to satisfy their need for money. They bring their own food for the duration of their stay. They can be met along the road, walking one behind the other, in file. The adults carry pots and supplies on their heads and often a child in the crook of the arm. It is not a case of aimless wandering. The migrants go directly to addresses where they have been before and old contacts send them on to possible new employers. They do not migrate for an indefinite time but for a few weeks only, until the grain brought with them is exhausted. The gang then returns home, to make the same journey again somewhat later in the season, with the same or other people. Arrangements made long beforehand and sometimes sealed with a cash advance, contribute to the fairly tight rhythm that characterises seasonal migration. This is a tidal flow that largely escapes the sight of outsiders.

These migratory groups, which include the Khandeshis, who travel for cane-cutting are reputed to be very hardworking. They do this heavy work on the orders of sugar co-operatives in the central plain, which contract them for the entire season. When all the fields in the neighbourhood have been harvested, they move their bivouac on to the next village. In this way they spend the period between early November and the end of May rotating over the canefields which are under the command of the sugar factories. The owners of mango and chiku orchards too are assured of the services of Dangis, tribals from the Dangs district, who arrive after the rainy season and stay until the end of summer. The number of these migrants is so large that, according to landowners, the supply of agricultural labourers available locally increases by one-fifth to one-quarter during that time.

Such migration is thus common, despite the widespread notion that the market for agrarian labour is distinctly local in character. Even the widespread evidence of the migration of agricultural labour does not convince those who accept the stereotypes of the Indian village and hold 'that the agricultural labour market is closed, in that the hiring of labour across neighbouring villages is rare. Each village is an enclave. One reason employers may not wish to hire workers from a different village is that they are unknown commodities. Hiring them

▼ **The temporary night shelters are nothing more than mats held up by poles and are so small that not all members of the *koyta* can be accommodated. Adults sleep in the open around the camp**

▶ **Children of the migrants do not go to school and are therefore condemned be to not only illiterate but also migrants themselves for the rest of their working lives**

would involve large risks; "foreign" workers may be unreliable, or simply incompetent.'

The quantitative and qualitative evidence pertaining to south Gujarat of course tells a different story. Indeed, this phenomenon is manifest in other regions as well. Labour mobility, both rural–urban and intra-rural, is indeed a widespread trend in the South Asian subcontinent. The inflow and outflow of migrants is part and parcel of a more general pattern of wage labour circulation. A recent survey of labour migration at the all-India level links the growing significance of

this phenomenon with increasing disparities that mark the process of economic development in various parts of the country. It identifies the rural army of unskilled and illiterate labour as being landless or land-poor from the agricultural–economic point of view, and as members of Scheduled Castes/Tribes or Other Backward Classes from the social perspective. Acute poverty forces these people to leave their villages, at least for a part of the year and frequently even longer.

Gujarat is identified as a state in which this process has developed to a considerable extent. Seasonal migration in various regions of

Gujarat is now an integral part of the lives of the landless. Labour mobility in the countryside of south Gujarat has become the rule rather than the exception and it has resulted in further degradation of labour which is most evident in the case of the cane-cutters.

The gang of cane-cutters, led by a jobber, which stays in the plain of south Gujarat for the sugarcane harvest is made up of twenty to fifty members. They are subdivided into smaller units, called *koytas*, usually made up of a man, woman and often a child. At the start of the working day the gang boss lines up the *koytas* at the beginning of the field. The members of each team have to cut the rows of stalks in front of them, remove the leaves, cut them into pieces, bundle them and carry them in headloads to the roadside. The area that all cover working in this way is the same, but the tempo depends on the labour power. This means that one work gang will finish its daily task earlier than another.

The norm is high: approximately two-thirds to three-quarters of a ton, which demands an effort lasting nine to ten hours. Weak teams need so much time that the gang boss may decide to transfer part of their task, and its payment, to other teams that have extra capacity. The norm is based on an uninterrupted workload, of which only the strong are capable. Those who have difficulty in keeping to that tempo and

in maintaining it until the end of the day are discharged in due course. They have been judged and found inadequate, unsuited to take further part in the production process.

Day and night, a fleet of vehicles — lorries, trucks and bullock carts — comes and goes, carrying cane to the factory. The factory management is in constant contact with the fieldstaff so as to accelerate the work if the supply is insufficient and to slow it down if the factory becomes congested. Cane-cutting has to be interrupted repeatedly because of machine defects in the mill, transport breakdowns, or other technical flaws. This means that on the one hand the army of cutters

has to be constantly available, but on the other hand it is not paid when breakdowns occur in the process. The vertically integrated organisation of agro-industry forces cane-cutters to load at night the amount of cane that they have cut during the day, because the mill's machines run continuously.

In cane-cutting, daily production is highest between November and February. From then on the amount of cane cut by a *koyta* drops to little more than half-a-ton every 24 hours. The heat during the day undoubtedly plays a role, but more important is the exhaustion caused by the production process itself. The decline in performance does not mean that working hours become any shorter. Only the effort put into the work slows down towards the end of the season.

The arms and hands of the cane-cutters are not protected against the knife-sharp top leaves or against slips with the machete. On their bare feet they have to carry their heavy headloads out of the stubble that they leave in the fields after harvesting. The primitive or even non-existent medical care means that wounds on arms and legs, hand and feet, easily become infected. As a result of the poor hygienic conditions under which seasonal migrants are forced to live, they often fall victim to chronic diseases such as dysentery, tuberculosis and malaria, and take them home. An impression of this can be gained from the following description of conditions found in cane-cutters' camps by a committee appointed by the High Court in Gujarat: 'Being compelled to use highly polluted, non-potable water for drinking purposes many a time, it is not surprising that there were large numbers of cases of workers suffering from dysentery and diarrhoea ... it was obvious that the workers live in total destitution without even a minimum facility for staying, clothing, and nothing to sleep on, children of tender age without clothes were a common sight at the camps. Pregnant and nursing mothers also sharing the same conditions, all left without any clothes to protect themselves from the winter cold.'

The women usually have to cope with a double burden of work. A few hours before starting their paid labour, they are busy with all sorts of domestic activities: preparing meals, caring for the children, washing and cleaning. They are the first to rise in the morning and the last to go to bed at night. The men come back tired from their work, demanding rest, care and attention. The women, who are equally tired, are expected as a matter of course to continue their work in the domestic sphere. It is hardly surprising then that the weakest members in their milieu are in turn victimised: 'If the children cry due to hunger, we beat them and force them to sleep. What else to do?'

There is bitterness behind the sweet taste of sugar.

9

THE BRICK MAKERS

Bricks have been manufactured in the Indian subcontinent for 5,000 years or more, ever since the Harappan civilisation. It is one of the ironies of history that it was the pillaging of bricks from an abandoned mound in order to use them as ballast for building a railway line that led to the discovery of the pre-historic Harappan civilisation. It was, as it were, one culture premised on industry and the technology of machines cannibalising an ancient urban predecessor based on commerce. What were common between the two cultures were bricks of a shape, size and quality — and brick manufacturing processes — that had changed little over the millennia that separated the two. Indeed, over the centuries, in most of India, fired or unfired mud-bricks have been the most commonly used building material for houses. And the demand for bricks is inexhaustible. In south Gujarat, for instance, there are far more brickyards now than two decades ago. And yet, there is not much literature available on these major rural industries which can be found in widely different parts of India.

◄ **The faster this little girl grows, the longer her arms will be, the more bricks she will carry (upto 14), and the higher the weekly advance she will receive. She yearns to grow up as soon as possible!**

A common feature of the brickyards is that they operate on a seasonal basis and seem to depend everywhere mainly on migrant labour. The brickfields in the south Gujarat region are situated mostly near the principal urban and industrial centres: between Surat and Navsari, on the road from Valsad to Vapi, and around Bilimora and Bardoli. The majority of these brickyards are not registered, and those located further from the roadside are not noticed by the passer-by. At the beginning of the 1960s, according to the Surat District Gazetteer, the industry provided work for approximately 3,000 workers in south

Gujarat for eight months per year. Even at that time, this must have heavily underestimated the workforce, whose size can now only be guessed at. In the 1990s, it was estimated that the region had at least 750 brickyards, each employing from forty to fifty workers (with considerable deviation on either side); i.e. a total workforce of some 30,000–40,000.

Brickyards can be divided into two categories, based primarily on the technology applied. *Bata* is the name given to small units whose owners do not need much starting capital. Land is the principal resource and has to be available in sufficient extent at or near the workplace. Cash advances then have to be made to hire an adequate supply of labour for the entire season. Finally, a number of other production costs have to be met: the possible digging of a well, the ordering of some truckloads of coal ash and rice husks. Adequate financial means, as also sound technical know-how of all manufacturing aspects, have to be available if the business is to run successfully. This is immediately put to the test in making a suitable choice of the work site, and is further shown in experience with production methods and work organisation. Understanding the market and knowledge of how to do business with customers are also prerequisites for successful entrepreneurship in this field.

The raw material is plain earth and water, producing just mud. The mud is mixed and kneaded, and a work gang consisting of nine to eleven men, women and children shapes bricks. The wet bricks are taken from the mould and left in rows to dry for some days. They are then piled tightly in alternate layers and coal ash is mingled with rice husk. This heap forms the oven, the actual *bata*, which is then fired.

When the pile of bricks has burned out and cooled off, the end product is ready for sale in the market. The oven thus consists of the bricks themselves and has to be built anew each time. The volume of the *bata* ranges to a maximum of 75,000 bricks. The time necessary to prepare this quantity varies with the number of work gangs, each producing 2,500–3,000 bricks per day.

Work in the second type of brickyard is similarly organised, but after the bricks have been formed and dried, they are taken to a fixed oval-shaped oven built round a chimney. Manufacture is both larger in scale and technologically more advanced. The oven, which has a capacity of 300,000–450,000 bricks, is divided into sections. While bricks are being baked in one or more of them, using coal as fuel, other sections are simultaneously being filled or emptied. The smaller type of establishment allows flexibility. Within the margins of his workforce, the owner can react to changing demand by making more *batas* or less, thus producing in accordance with the flow of sales. Greater overheads and the need to maintain a more equal rate of production entail that a big entrepreneur will only decide to build a chimney if sufficient raw material is available nearby and if a large and, above all, regular turnover is likely at the end of the production chain.

For the owner of a *bata*, the purchase of a lorry is of greater importance to his market position than a surge to greater volume, with all the risks that this implies. Buying a motored transport vehicle makes for easier access to the market and makes him less dependent on customers to come and collect the product themselves at the work site.

Most brickyard owners belong to local castes and have varying social backgrounds. The trade has great attraction for members of the Kumbhar (potters) caste who nowadays prefer to call themselves Prajapatis — after the mythological original creator of the universe — and mostly own small brickyards. The entrepreneurs owning chimneys include Parsis, Desais and members of other high castes. A few Koli Patels, clearly on their way up as industrialists, have invested in the brick-making industry after having earned the initial capital as contract labourers in the Gulf. Finally, an increasing number of owners come from Saurashtra in south Gujarat. Originally potters and members of related castes, they were attracted by the enormous growth of the building trade and production of building materials. Like the workers, these migrant entrepreneurs too return home at the end of the season.

The setting up of more and more brickyards in south Gujarat means that the marginal peasants and landless who form the workforce can now find employment close to home. Over the years, Halpatis and Dhodhiyas from the region who used to go to Mumbai to seek work, now find employment much nearer their villages; but not near enough to enable them to combine this seasonal work with living at home. Even if the brickyard is only 10–15 km from the village of the labourers, daily commuting is out of the question. Migrants who are employed within a 100–150 km radius of their homes may at most only occasionally return to their homes for brief breaks during a seven–eight month season.

The pattern of 'local' migration is illustrated by the following case: 'M is a widow and only allows herself to be recruited for brickyards that she can reach from her village in a fairly short time. That is because her two children have to stay in the village. The eight-year-old daughter is old enough to work together with her mother, but not the four-year-old son. Both thus stay at home where the girl looks after her little brother. The neighbours keep an eye on them. M returns home once a month to put affairs in order and to bring money for the coming

▶ **Women and donkeys do all the carrying of bricks from the kilns to the roadside for further transport. The total labour charge per brick is not more than 10 per cent of the sale price, while the profit for the owner comes close to 50 per cent**

'Do you have land in the village?' the brick-maker was asked. He said, pointing in front of him, 'This is my field, and the bricks are my harvest.'

weeks. This year she is working near Surat, and travelling back and forth is a heavy charge on her meagre budget. She leaves the brickyard early in the afternoon, reaches her village in the evening, and then stays until late the following afternoon. In this way she loses as little work as possible. On the other hand, she has no breathing space in which to recuperate. When she returns at the end of the season, M is worn out.'

The rapid expansion of the brick industry in south Gujarat has attracted hordes of workers from far-flung areas. This is partly due to the complicated division of work in large-scale enterprises. Certain activities are reserved for workers who are thought to have a special skill. For example, chimney stokers invariably come from Uttar Pradesh, while the transport of bricks at the work site from the drying place to the kiln and emptying the oven after the baking process, are entrusted to mule drivers from north Gujarat and Rajasthan. Even the brick-makers are increasingly brought from outside the region.

This preference for migrant labour is for reasons of industrial management. The local work gang of nine to eleven members, called *surthi*, after Surat, the name of the city as well as the district, is vulnerable. If even one worker is absent, the day's production falls. Employers try to counter this problem by replacing the *surthi*, wholly or partially, with Khandeshis from Maharashtra who work in teams of two or three. This system is sometimes called *hajaria*, which implies that a three-member team (man, woman and working child) account for the production of 1,000 bricks per day.

This explanation for preferring migrant labourers is, however, imperfect considering the fact that many migrants are also employed under the *surthi* method. It would perhaps be more logical to suggest that, due to the enormous expansion of the industry, the demand for labour is far greater than the local supply. But then this too lacks conviction, because the flow of migrants from central Gujarat (Vadodara, Anand) and Saurashtra to brickyards in the south of the state is countered by an outflow of similar labour, including Halpatis, to those places. Seasonal work and labour migration are obviously closely linked and both phenomena have to be understood in the light of their interacting dynamics.

In any event, a gang of brick-makers consisting of nine to eleven members, organised in the *surthi* pattern, is expected to produce and stack 2,500 to 3,000 bricks per day. The amount of earth and other raw materials (coal dust and rice husks) with which they are provided at the start of the workday is attuned to that number. The time in which the quickest and slowest gangs manage to process this quantity varies from ten to fourteen hours.

▼ **Women try to carry as many bricks as possible because payment is on a per piece basis. The load could easily be around 30 kgs**

Members of the brick-making gangs are labelled unskilled workers. What needs to be understood, however, is that from the beginning till the end the division of labour is organised as an assembly-line production

There is little technology but a considerable amount of skill involved in brick-making. Earth is dug up and brought by truck, tractor or donkey to the brickyard. Members of the gang who are charged with the transport of earth use only a spade as the tool of their trade in dealing with *mati*. Often enough, large clumps are passed by hand or headload. On the work site, the earth is distributed in piles at the places where the brick-making gangs are at work. The amount needed for a day's production is thrown into a pit filled

with water. Then two or three men chosen for the task mix the earth with water, coal dust and rice husk. They knead the mixture for hours with legs and hands, standing in the pit from which they remove stones, bits of wood and other flotsam. Two other men and/or women dig the resulting mash out of the pit with their hands and knead it once again. Then the partner of the brick-maker squatting next to the pile, seizes a ball of mud with both hands and passes it to the *patawala* who puts it into the mould. This linchpin of the group then smoothes both sides of the mould, an action that he has to repeat 2,500 to 3,000 times a day. When the mould is shifted off, the wet clay remains in the form of a brick on the steel groundplate. Two or three children, depending on their age, then take turns to lift the plate with the brick and run with it to an older child who carefully lays the bricks next to one another. The rows that are thus formed are left to dry for half-a-day. But then the occupied space has to be emptied for the next series. Members of the same gang carry the bricks a little further away to pile them in rows so that the drying process can continue. Another work gang, almost all girls and women, then carry eight or ten bricks together on their heads to the kiln, where they are taken over by one or two men who specialise in the correct stacking of the half-product for the firing process. They also take the fired bricks out of the oven and pass them to the waiting women bearers. These women then carry their heavy headload to the stockpile from where the end product is transported away, or directly to a waiting truck.

Gangs that systematically fail to produce the required number of bricks are penalised for their shortcomings by a reduction of the weekly allowance on which they depend for their sustenance. The norm is based on an uninterrupted workload, of which only the strong are capable. Those who have difficulty in keeping to that tempo and in maintaining it until the end of the day are discharged in due course.

During the period that they are employed, not only adults but children too are victims of the miserable working conditions in the brickworks. The production organisation of the brickworks is such that the labour power of children becomes indispensable while they are still quite young, and from the age of six they are wakened during the night to carry the fresh bricks made by their father. While wet, those bricks weigh roughly three kilos. The little children run with one brick each, away from the base plate and into the darkness. When they reach the age of about nine, they are promoted to carrying two bricks.

Sometimes their parents wake them up crying from the rags that form their beds. But at night they are the only ones who sing, trying to give themselves courage. If they run back quickly they can warm their hands for a few seconds by the wood fire which provides the *patawala* and *patawali*, the brick-maker and his female mate, with light and warmth in the cold winter nights.

The following notes from a research field diary illustrate the conditions in the brickworks: 'Last night, while the parents were at work, a

toddler was badly burned. The little boy, not yet three years old, had scampered to the kiln to seek warmth. There he must have fallen against the hot bricks in his sleep. Wet rags did little to stop the lad's screaming and crying... A couple of days later, in another brickworks, I found a girl of about fifteen years old who lay on the ground under a couple of jute sacks, shivering with fever. Her younger sister came now and again and shook her gently, trying to get her to go to work, because she was unable alone to carry all the bricks away from the base plate. The labour power of her sick sister is needed to eliminate the backlog. When that has been done, she can lie down again although for no longer than ten minutes.'

In the brickworks, precautionary occupational health or even first aid measures of any kind are conspicuous by their absence. Injuries of all kinds are common occurrences in the handling of raw materials, operating the kiln and humping the bricks in the successive processing stages. The workers who stand in the mixing pits for hours at a time, the women who carry the bricks on their heads twelve or fourteen at a time with a total weight of about twenty-five to thirty kilos, the brick-maker and his partner who sit in a squatting posture for hours on end — they all complain about pain in their backs and other parts of the body. Workers point out the many knock-kneed children, a defect that is

certainly caused by a combination of poor food, long working hours, and too heavy burdens at a young age. Brown lung disease seems to be another complaint peculiar to this branch of industry. It applies particularly to the *chapawali*, the women who each day and all day carry the baked bricks out of the kiln. By evening their faces are like masks, entirely covered in dust. Using an edge of their *sari* they do their best to cover their mouth and nostrils. But the stone dust even penetrates that veil.

A well-known doctor in Valsad has his medical practice in a neighbourhood populated by unskilled labourers. He attributes the poor health of the majority of his patients to the conditions under which they have to work: 'How will they be able to do normal work when they have to inhale dust particles? They take cold and insufficient food. Over and above that they consume liquor to relieve themselves of tensions and exhaustion. Their lungs become weak and they begin to suffer from incurable diseases like TB and asthma. They suffer from sunstroke, as they have to work in a scorching heat. There are some cases of cholera too. They suffer from boils because they sit in dirty,

◀ **Women kneading earth with water and rice husk. All wages are settled at the end of the season, when the workers are sent off**

insanitary places. Some female labourers are compelled to have sexual relations with people in order to get work and other favours. That leads to venereal diseases.'

The brutal labour regime imposes an even heavier burden on women and children than on men. Boys and girls of 10–12 years of age frequently have to work the same long hours as the adults, but at their tender age they are less able to withstand fatigue. Their pace of strenuous work is not always adequate, and it is quite customary for employers and overseers to be harsh in disciplining them. Their greater vulnerability makes them an easy target for verbal or physical violence and for the continual threat of dismissal due to default.

In the brickyards, as elsewhere, working girls and women run the risk of sexual abuse. This may be forced on them by the *mukadam* who can select or ignore them for employment, by an employer or his foreman who can dismiss them if they refuse a wide range of sexual intimacies or resist rape. Usually the only protest possible against such treatment is to leave the workplace. And that option is not open to them in a system of subordination practised by employers, gang bosses and the male heads of labouring households.

10

BUILDERS AND DIGGERS

Among the hordes of migrants who settle on the urban periphery, many are to be found on building sites. Their incursions into the city are brief, lasting no more than a few weeks or months. Once the job for which they have been taken on is completed, they return home like many informal sector workers who cannot afford the luxury of specialising in any particular trade and who more frequently circulate through various stations of employment.

There are others who come for longer periods and have found shelter in one of the city's many seedy quarters. They undertake all kinds of odd jobs for a multiplicity of employers, whether as wage labour, on a sub-contracting basis, or on their own account and risk. Their precarious existence in the urban arena is based on casual work and diverse sources of income.

Both these types of workers are referred to as slum dwellers, having set up extremely temporary or semi-permanent abodes in the shadow of the city's skyscrapers. As unauthorised squatters, they have invaded private or public land which is not their own. The only hope of the

▲ **Women are reduced to being heasts of burden. They are invariably only the 'helpers' of men**

illegal occupants is that their colonies will be regularised after some time. However, slum-dwellers are a removable lot and many such city residents have been evicted more than once. The threat of eviction remains a prime concern in this milieu, as is evident from this case study of a Surat slum: '...the people do not have any individual permission or something to certify that they are legal residents of this place, such as a house tax, ration card, etc. Hence, even if people want to improve their house they don't do it because it can be destroyed at any time. (Such people) are caught up in a dilemma: they cannot leave the place for another as it is unavailable and at the same time cannot build a *pucca* house. People feel that it is better for them to invest in a good house back in their village.'

Both space for a tenement and the material to build it are difficult to come by for the urban poor. The slum is not an open arena nor does everybody have free access to the waste that is lying around. There are regular traders who deal in recycled plastics, asbestos or corrugated iron sheets, rejected bricks, old wood, etc. and there are specialised workers using such second-hand material for the construction of all kinds of slum dwellings. Housing conditions such as these explain why circulation remains such an important feature in the life and work of the very large part of Surat's population which is down and out in the informal sector.

The irony is that many such workers are enaged in the construction industry building houses, roads and other parts of the urban infrastructure for the use of the higher segments of society.

The building and repair of roads is a speciality of tribal labour originating from the Panch Mahals in central Gujarat, and of the

orders and stay with them throughout the season. The *mukadams* rove through all of Gujarat together with the contractors, but their work gangs differ each year in composition.

The manner of building even primary roads demands some degree of training: laying the gravel, pouring the asphalt; a few skilled workers operate the tar-spreading machine, steamroller, etc. This division of labour does not apply to

Kathiawadis from the western peninsula of the state. The composition of this workforce is now more diverse than in the past. Over the years, recruitment has been extended to other regions. However, a very large segment of such labourers continues to comprise tribal Bhils from the Panch Mahals.

The men do skilled work; the women and children act as their helpers. They eat and sleep along the roadside, in a bivouac that moves as work progresses. The group is generally divided into two gangs of up to fifty workers each, led by a foreman or *mukadam*.

These *mukadams* recruit their gang members on the contractor's

workers who widen or harden country roads on the orders of local builders, but even they are often seasonal migrants from other regions. The description of a typical repair work of a country road reads: 'The road is closed for repairs. On both sides, down the slopes, men are breaking the ground with pickaxes. Women carry away the clods of earth in iron pans. They clamber with their headloads up the verge to where others stand ready to spread the material over the road surface and to pulverize it. There is no machinery, which perhaps explains why there are so many people. Four foremen — *mukadams* or labour contractors — are in charge of gangs totalling 200 workers. Two-thirds of these come from Saurashtra, the remainder from Dharampur in the eastern hills of south Gujarat. The former belong to the untouchable Vankar caste, the latter are tribal Kuknas. The work is paid on a piece-work basis and is carried out by the entire family. Each day the *mukadam* measures the ground that has been covered by each

work team. That amount is the basis for their payment, depending on the total labour power of husband, wife and children. Each week they are paid an advance, calculated on the amount of work done, with which to meet their primary necessities. The balance that remains after deduction of such advances and loans is not paid out until the end of the season. The contractor cannot keep them for long. Everyone wants to return to the village to cultivate the land before the first rains fall. Once they reach home, they at least have a roof over their heads. There they can also enjoy the intimacy of family life. Here, everything has to be done in the open field — not only cooking and sleeping, but also having sex or quarrelling with one another.'

Even such a rude existence is dependent on the availability of a raw material: stone. Stone is needed not only for road construction but also for the foundations of all buildings, and is quarried in numerous places throughout south Gujarat. Since the early years of the 1970s,

▶ **It will take a long time for the low technology of road building in the rural areas to be replaced with capital-intensive equipment**

most quarries have been exploited by private concessionaries. Previously, only the Public Works Department obtained stone from the quarries. The development of the region's infrastructure necessitated a greater volume of material, however, and more and more contractors started to open up their own quarries. Many such quarry contractors are road builders who operate on a small scale.

The quarries are located next to one another and each employs about fifty men and women. They are mostly Dhodhiyas and some Halpatis, marginal peasants and landless people from the surrounding villages who come in the morning and return home at night. Opencast mining means that work has to be stopped in the rainy season. This is convenient, however, because these small peasants are then engaged in growing crops. The workers report back again only after having harvested paddy in October.

The method of extraction is very simple, depending chiefly on manual labour. The only machine is a compressor, which provides the power necessary to drill holes in the rock face. Dynamite is then placed in the holes and exploded. The quarrymen wrench loose chunks of rock which they then break up with sledgehammers. Their wives carry these smaller lumps to a level stretch of land where they and the children hammer them to pieces. This is all done on a piece-work basis, paid per *brass,* i.e. the contents of a filled bin equalling a weight of four tons. Two such bins fill the trucks in which the crushed stone is taken away.

Looking down the hill from above, all that can be noticed is a

crawling mass of hundreds of men, women and children all working together in family groups. In each quarry a contractor's agent keeps an eye on production and administers its progress.

There are also cases where contractors prefer to hire migrant rather than local labour for the quarries because, in their opinion, the local workers are no good: 'They report for work very irregularly and stay away for days or even weeks at a time. The migrants are satisfactory.' The migrant workers live at the worksite and, if only for that reason, are readily available throughout the season.

Some mechanisation of production is also taking place in the quarries. There is increasing deployment of equipment operated by two men which can do the work for which nearly 100 men and women were previously needed. Stone production has become big business, an extension of scale emphasised by transfer of the concessions to large entrepreneurs who contract projects throughout all of western India. To save on transport costs, they exploit a number of quarries situated as close as possible to their various work sites. Trucks go back and forth; tractors with excavator buckets remove the topsoil and open up the hillside at two or three levels. The rock face is punctured with pneumatic drills. The increase in capital intensity in such quarrying has brought about a complicated division of work and a prolonged

season. Work is only halted when rainfall is heavy, to be resumed immediately afterwards on the top level which is least affected by flooding.

This change in the work pattern has also resulted in the complete replacement of local labourers by migrant workers. The specialised machine operators all belong to higher castes and enjoy formal conditions of employment. This does not, however, apply to the manual workers who set up camp — a collection of huts made of reed mats — on the open plain at the bottom of the quarry. They are mostly members of low castes from Sholapur in Maharashtra, while others come all the way from Karnataka. They have been working in the same quarry for some years now, brought in by the same contractor for whom they had done road-building work nearer their home village. The male stone-hewers and their female helpers together with working children are divided into gangs led by a *thekadar*. These gang bosses are responsible for recruitment in the home area as well as for supervising the work.

Many changes have taken place in the quarry south of Valsad, of which Western Railways is a major and regular customer. The owner of the formerly modest quarry spent a great deal of money on technological improvements in order to meet the rapidly growing demand for stone. For example, he installed movable rails along which stone could be brought in tilting carts from the quarry up the hill and down to the road, and an air pressure pipe runs upwards to the top of the hill to power the pneumatic drills. Production is now stopped for just two months during the monsoon, and that is only because work is hindered by flooding. It is not stopped in order that local workers may devote themselves to agricultural work. They are no longer needed since the coming of migrants from Khandesh in western Maharashtra. Elsewhere in India also, surprisingly, long-distance work migrants often operate stone quarries. The workforce for opencast mining in Madhya Pradesh, for example, originates in Tamil Nadu. Enterprises in Haryana use migrants from Madhya Pradesh, Maharashtra, Rajasthan and Bihar. Similarly, many road-building gangs in Tripura and Kashmir come from as far away as Bihar and Orissa and these often comprise bonded labourers taken from their home states by contractors to face unfamiliar conditions ranging from terrorism to frostbite.

▶ **A report by a senior civil servant on the working and living conditions of quarry and stone crushers states: 'The workers themselves are not free to come and give a statement before an outsider as they are constantly living under a psychosis of fear and insecurity both at the place of work and stay.'**

At the same time, while changes have taken place in these segments of the informal sector in terms of the expanding universe of labour recruitment and even some mechanisation, nothing much seems to have changed with regard to the quality of the workers' life. The open-air existence of these workers is extremely miserable, without even the most basic amenities. Their employers, however, frequently disagree. The manager of a sugar mill was quite convinced that the much lower wage paid to fieldworkers was compensated by their stay in the countryside: 'During the campaign they live in similar fashion to the sort of picnicking and camp life that westerners enjoy in leisure

time', he commented.

Life in the stone quarries is harsh. The workers who quarry the hills in the middle of the plain do not even have water nearby in which they can once in a while seek cooling during the hot summer months. The workers in the open air are perhaps less exposed to modern industrial pollution than are the factory workers, but they run other risks that may result in temporary or permanent harm to the body. Industrial accidents are a common occurrence on work locations in the informal sector. Building sites in particular are notorious for risks to which casual workers are exposed. The contractor refuses to accept any liability for injuries resulting in temporary or even permanent disability, and it is equally futile for the worker to seek redress from the *mukadam*. On the contrary, it is quite normal for the victim to be instantly dismissed without any form of compensation.

Men and women frequently fall victim to the primitive modes of extraction that are still practised in the majority of quarries: 'The feet and lower legs are particularly at risk because the labourers work with bare feet and legs. The greatest risks occur when large rocks have to be hacked into more manageable pieces with a sledgehammer; the pieces are rolled into position and held there with the bare feet. There is always a great danger of rebounding hammers and mis-hits.'

Workers dive down to the bottom of the highly polluted Tapti river downstream from Surat city to dredge and scoop up pans of sand for use in the construction industry. Their 'catch' is brought in small boats and carried ashore by women on their heads. They work from early morning till late evening and break their work rhythm with songs. In those songs they sarcastically praise the mercy of the bosses who enticed them there, far from home, with their cash advances.

Life under the open skies is anything but a picnic. It can be nasty, brutish and short for those who produce the raw materials for the construction industry. From the earth, stone and sand procured by an army of builders and diggers, cities like Mumbai, Surat and Ahmedabad are built, mixed with the sweat of these men, women and children.

11

OFF WORK

A woman's work is never over: she never goes off work. In the brick and cane fields as well as in the city slums where informal sector work takes place, women wake up before dawn: to scavenge for fuel, collect water, prepare food for the family. And, after performing these unpaid household chores, in many cases they join their menfolk in poorly paid employment. When the 'outside' work is done, they return to the domestic jobs again, slogging on to keep the family going, till absolute tiredness takes them to a few hours of sleep. So exhausting is their routine that it is a wonder they dare to dream at all.

Many informal sector men too yearn for sleep. Long working hours — often protracted voluntarily to earn some piteous extra-time payment or to supplement income by working on a second job — combine with poor living conditions to deprive them of rest. The thousands of migrant powerloom workers in Surat from faraway Orissa, for instance, live in community dormitories. One of them, generally one who is too old to find work on the machines, is 'employed' to cook for the group that hires the communal abode, often just a miserable room in a city slum. There the workers hang their personal belongings on pegs and store 'valuables' in battered tin trunks or, increasingly, in moulded plastic suitcases, and take turns to snatch sleep, much-required after working long shifts on the looms.

◀ **Powerloom workers at the end of their 12-hour shift, packed like sardines in a single room. They get up to be replaced in their sleeping space by the members of the next shift**

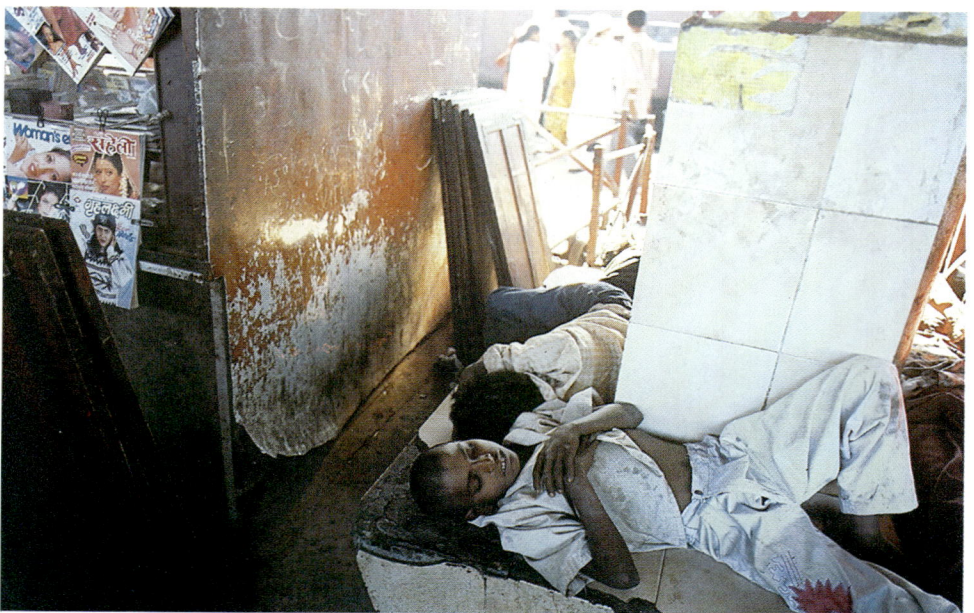

There are others, even less fortunate, for whom sleep deprivation is even more acute. When their bodies can take it no more, they collapse where they are — on pavements, on noisy railway platforms and over-bridges, even on carts and boats in the heat of the sizzling sun — in senseless slumber. And they are back on their feet the moment their labour power is on call again

Even during wakefulness, there is little that is 'off work' among such people. There is, in actual fact, unconditional surrender to the labour process during night and day, winter and summer. Work is total and it is practically impossible to assert 'off work' autonomous time. There are also the compulsions of the highly irregular nature of the labour process; these necessitate simply hanging around, waiting for work, being at the beck and call of the employer. These also mean keeping healthy even in the miserable conditions of life for illness means loss of wages. The reserve army of labour must remain fit for it is never known when the reserves may be called upon. Life itself is lived in the shadow

of work and there is little that can be described as leisure. Thus, brief breaks for rest have to be snatched away from the eyes of the employer or his agent.

Such leisure as there is revolves round food, sex, fantasy and religion. Hurried sips of tea from a saucer while wary eyes look out for the employer; a meal quickly put together by the wife, the commune cook preparing meals — these are some of the dominant images of 'leisure' time activity.

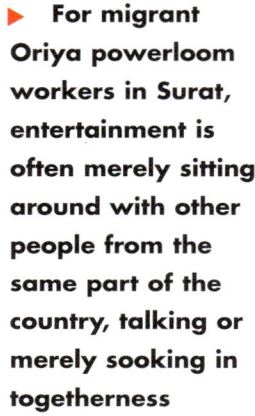

▼ **A diamond worker escapes from the daily grind of polishing minute stones with painful concentration, and spends money at a street-side fair**

▶ **For migrant Oriya powerloom workers in Surat, entertainment is often merely sitting around with other people from the same part of the country, talking or merely sooking in togetherness**

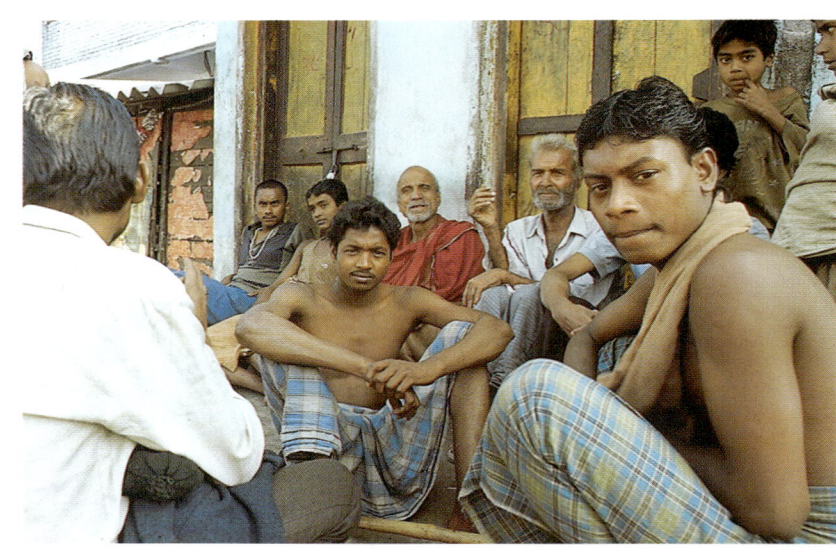

In such circumstances, some leisure activities may appear mundane and others bizarre.

Religion, rituals and the celebration of religious festivals are important 'off work' activities. It is interesting that even street entertainers don garbs of deities to beg for alms; they know that among a people for whom religion is so significant — not only as the 'opium of the masses' but also, despite the superstitious practices that go along with it, as a healing factor — the sacred command commercial currency too.

violence is only skin-deep in the slums with the tensions of the workplace and harsh life ever ready to burst out like a sore. There is thus wife beating and child abuse, alcoholism and drug addiction as well as all manners of self and social degradation. There is always the undercurrent of violence: rivalries and fights among workers, terror of bootleggers and slumlords, high-pitched quarrels among women waiting at the municipal taps for water. If there are instances of solidarity and comradeship, there are also many examples of aggression, jealousy, competition and even enmity.

There are also the seasonal festivals, celebrated differently by different communities hailing from different regions. These constitute a calendar that provides much-needed breaks in the dreary routine of the daily grind. It is another matter that even the celebration of the supernatural on occasion results in an outburst of passion and of violence. Many communal riots start from trivial quarrels. It is as if

▲ **Holi is an event which is more than festive. Gangs of young males go around to demonstrate their machoness aggressively and often enough the results are slum quarrels, street fights and even communal clashes**

total lack of privacy under which most such workers live and toil in the countryside as well as in the cities often deprives them of even this basic need. There is thus the crucial difference between having a roof, however makeshift, over the head and to live in the street, on the roadside or in the fields without protection and without privacy. This is a difference which is often not taken into account, particularly by those employers who extol the 'advantages of healthy open-air living', little realising the degradation that the workers in such circumstances have to suffer.

But then there is cinema, the fantasy machine, the favourite mode of relaxation. In some respects, popular culture itself appears to be existing under the domination of mass cinema. For workers whose real life holds little appeal, the tantalising images that flash on the silver screen provide sublimation, even as they widen the base of consumerism and thereby doubly serve the needs of capital and commerce.

But the short periods of fantasy purchased in cinema houses or even the temporary 'high' brought on by gambling cannot really substitute for the harshness of life in the informal sector. Take sex. The

▶ **The sex worker, engaged in one of the best paid professions in the informal sector**

nature: homosexuality thus is not a matter of sexual preference but is mere sodomy, a substitute for 'normal sex' among men forced to spend long periods just among themselves, in a cruel world where the young become prey for the old hands. The relatively more affluent diamond workers seek sexual sublimation though blue films that are shown in the ateliers at night and in that context male rape is not unheard of.

But even in these elemental conditions, there is joy and the celebration of nature, of companionship and even of the climate.

Even other workers, better equipped in that respect, suffer their own quotas of deprivation. Male migrant workers in cities, living for long periods away from their families, lead lonely lives even in the crowded communal dormitories that they inhabit. Recourse to commercialised sex is their way of satisfying a fundamental urge and consequently red light areas and sex workers come into existence wherever there is a concentration of single male workers. The cosmetic allure that is a part of such sex for sale cannot hide the fact that the world of commercial sex is ugly, dirty and often dangerously diseased. The ugliness of sex in these circumstances is enhanced by its forced

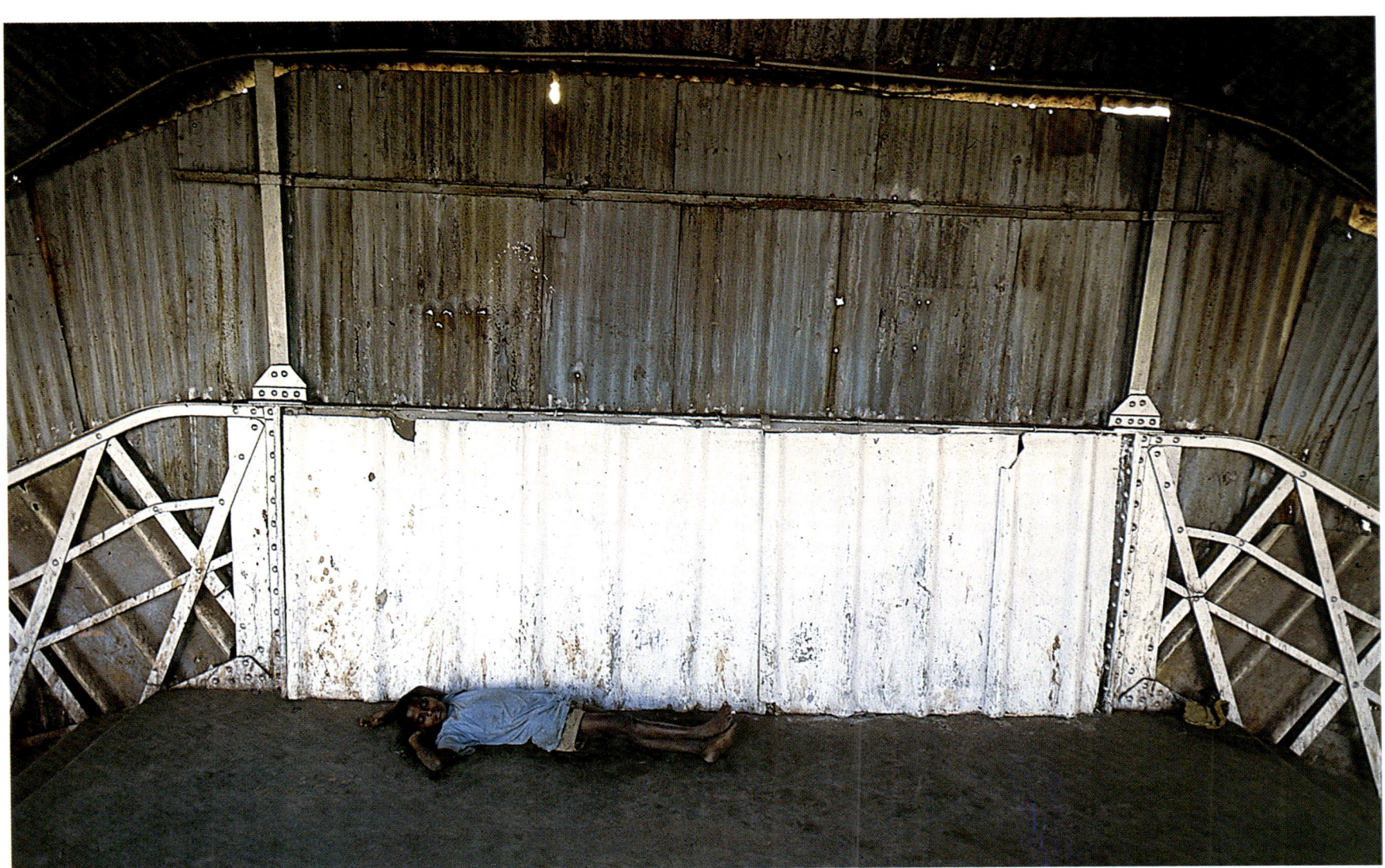

12

THE ASSERTION OF DIGNITY

After investigating labour in its totality, it has been concluded by a morphologist of the Indian working class and its labouring poor that 'the organised/unorganised boundary is not a wall but a steep slope. Indian society is like a mountain, with the very rich at the top, lush Alpine pastures where skilled workers in the biggest modern industries graze, a gradual slope down through smaller firms where pay and conditions are worse and legal security of employment means less, a steep slope around the area where the Factories Act ceases to apply, a plateau where custom and market give poorly paid unorganised sector workers some minimal security, then a long slope through casual migrant labour and petty services to destitution'.

This picture of labour demolishes the myth of duality and does suggest that there exists a labour continuum. However, it also implies that it is a dismal scene at the bottom of the heap, a scene that can only evoke despair. That is true to a large extent. There is vulnerability,

And once children are born, they have to be tended till they in turn start earning. There is thus the burden of 'unproductive' children, which has to be borne by the parents, particularly by mothers. There is also the burden of old age. In a society where there is no institutional old age care worth the name, the only social security is through the family. Adults look after children and the children, when they grow up, in turn care for

▲ **A pregnant women continues to lift heavy loads. Production dominates even reproduction**

irregularity, insecurity and indignity of living at the bottom. Often the only escape for the poor is by passing out in a state of drunkenness. Even this outlet is, however, available only to men. Women can not afford to opt out because of their reproductive role. They have the dual burden of looking after their families after doing paid work outside. The pregnant woman in the brick kiln carrying a heavy head load of bricks, for instance, has no leisure even for pre-natal rest.

the elderly. Thus is the social relay race run at the bottom of the labour pyramid.

The image of the pyramid should suggest no grandness. Despite the fact that labour of this sort is essential to sustain the kind of society that obtains, the prevailing image of labour is that of a nuisance. It is one of unwelcome filthy people, stinking from sweat and despair, illegally squatting on land and being evicted from time to time. It is one of dirt, disease and squalor. Hence, often enough the municipal authorities attempt to 'clean up' the cities by removing the working poor out of sight.

The contrasting images on advertisement hoardings too cannot detract from the fact that dignity exists even within the squalor of existence on the streets. Indeed, the fantasy images on hoardings and the consumerism peddled through posters, the exaggerated emotions articulated through film songs and festivals — all these open up spaces for the labouring poor, spaces in which to escape from the dreariness of daily life. In the most dingy homes, pride in the simplest of possessions is another expression of the same human dignity since a 'decent' house, regular life, adequate caring for the aged and the young, acceptable work conditions are the objects of striving through the grind of work.

But human beings have an infinite capacity to alter situations, to

carve out autonomous spaces, to assert the dignity of the individual, enhance mutuality within the family and ensure group solidarity even in the most adverse circumstances.

Such manifestation of human dignity may take very simple forms. It may be merely through snatching a few moments of leisure from work, cuddling an infant, standing erect even after performing back-breaking work. It may also show itself in the innocent smiles of children, in the little games they devise for themselves in the worst situations, in the uninhibited spurt of happiness that occasionally visits even pavement dwellers. Simple acts of caring for and caressing each other, snatching fleeting moments of intimacy in the threatening urban jungle, creating niches of privacy even while being forced to live their lives constantly on the public platform — all these are minor but nevertheless significant.

There is the assertion of individual as well as social dignity — *izzat* — through simple acts of

▲ **Children living on the streets and railway stations often come from broken homes and are exposed to sexual abuse. They eat the leftovers from the meals served to the passengers**

citizenship. The exercising of the right of the citizen, howsoever poor and oppressed, to cast his or her vote endows the labourer with power even though such democratic power is exercised only occasionally. Empowerment is also sought and achieved through local-level organisations, through group activity, and through literacy.

It is also significant that the poverty that is manifest is quite often the poverty of development, not of backwardness and stagnation. Surat and its hinterland, just like Gujarat at large, exist in the global context of fairly rapid growth, predatory capitalism and the on-going informalisation of the economy. But this itself implies the journey from exclusion to inclusion, from despair to hope, from degradation to dignity in a noticeable but nevertheless silent manner.

But the assertion of the dignity of labour and resistance to exploitation can also take other forms. These too need not be dramatic and flamboyant: there are many modes of everyday resistance — from malingering to carrying out deliberate acts of sabotage — enabling the labouring poor to get their own back against exploitation, abuse, oppression and even the torture that they are subjected to by employers.

In the worst of situations, workers simply vote with their feet: they run away and seek employment with other employers and in other activities. They are then seen to act 'irrationally', i.e. to simply abscond when they feel that enough is enough or when they take time out when employers and their agents concede no rest. There are also many instances when casual workers insist on piece-work. Such sub-contracting leads to self-exploitation but, at the same time, work on

specific logic and its own sanctions: the civil order of the formal sector *vis-à-vis* the tacit anarchy that is supposed to be the destiny of that part of humankind which is 'unorganised'. It is not recognised that there are distinct social solidarities even among the most 'unorganised', the most fragment sections of societies. These links of solidarity and mutual support may at times be based on extra-economic relationships like caste. The Dalits among the informal sector

▶ **Caste and class solidarities come together in this small union focussing on Dalit workers, operating under the legacy of B.R. Ambedkar**

one's own account and even the attendant risk has another and more emancipatory aspect.

It is also important to remember that collective action too is not unknown in the informal sector. A mistaken dichotomy is often applied to society in accordance with the bifurcation of the economy into a formal and an informal sector. The parallel duality is supposed to rest on two separate systems of existence, each with its own

workers, for instance, often get together not so much on a class basis — under the traditional red flag, as it were — but with inspiration drawn from the great Dalit lawgiver, Dr B. R. Ambedkar, under their own distinctive blue flag. But whether they carry the red flag or the blue one when they proclaim their strike even on fleeting media like moving trains, the finformal sector labouring poor reach out to the workforce higher up in the economic landscape.

There has been a great deal of debate on what constitutes class: Parsonian pedants have gone down with much conceptual huffing and puffing to the engine room of society to find class in this or that part of the machine. They have not been able to find it particularly when they have looked at the seemingly anarchic parts that constitute the informal sector. The fact is that class is not any specific part but the very action of the machine, the friction, the heat, the thundering noise. And class manifests itself in many ways, all modes of resistance, assertion of autonomy and establishing dignity.

It is in this context that the Social Darwinistic notion of such workers constituting a 'dangerous class' takes root in the elite since such labourers are automatically equated with the lumpen proletariat. The existence of violence within and among segments of this workforce reinforces suspicion and fear regarding it. There is a lurking idea that even such an 'unorganised sector' may experience a sudden and violent groundswell and erupt one day, wrecking the established order.

◀ **Even commodities have names. A powerloom worker, on a gruelling twelve hour shift sweats it out in the heat and noise of an atelier**

EPILOGUE

BY ARVIND N. DAS

first met Jan Breman in Banmankhi in Purnea district of north-eastern Bihar in the late 1970s. We were holding a Rural Labour Camp and he had been invited to represent the International Labour Organisation there. His recently published book, *Patronage and Exploitation*, had appeared to us to be relevant to the situation in which we were holding the Camp. We had assembled about fifty agricultural labourers and were attempting to educate them about laws relevant to them that existed on the statute books, and about the advantages of setting up their own organisations. We ourselves were just learning of the cruel realities of bondage and clientilism in villages.

Our entire discourse was then confined within the framework of employment and income in the agricultural sector. The mere possibility of rural but non-agricultural work did not occur to us despite the fact that the Camp itself was being held in one of the outhouses belonging to a sugar mill where hundreds of labourers toiled. We were still prisoners of the supposed dichotomy between rural and urban, agricultural and industrial, unorganised and organised sectors. The relative passivity of the working class in the upsurges of the late 1960s and the contrasting intensity of peasant activism formed the empirical basis on which the edifices of many of our theories were erected. Maoist ideas of agrarian revolutionism combined with those of 'the aristocracy of unionised labour'. Proletarianism was out-moded; insurrectionism was in.

Those were the years when peasant wars were raging in Latin America, when peasant guerrillas were defeating the Americans in Vietnam, when the embers of agrarian Naxalism glowed in India itself. Those were also the years of the fossilisation of the trade union movement, of the formulation of 'Garibi Hatao' policies, of the fragmentation by the Robert McNamara-led World Bank of workers into the formal and informal sectors. Those were the best of times; those were also the worst of times.

It was in such a situation — and in a rural labour camp where many of the participants were extremely poor landless agricultural workers belonging to the Musahar caste, members of which still survive on the field mice they manage to catch — that Jan Breman came in. He brought with him experience both of the deprivations suffered by the working class in Europe till the Second World War as well as of the dynamics of the prosperous social democratic society and the welfare state created since then. At the same time, he also brought to the camp in Bihar the knowledge that he had gathered during more than a decade of fieldwork among the labourers of south Gujarat: the transformation of the Kaliparaj 'black-skinned' Hali bonded into Halpatis, the changing forms of bondage, attachment and other forms of employment of labour, and the slowly but surely altering forms of self-perception among the untouchables, from the traditional 'untouchable' through the Gandhian Harijan (children of God) to 'Dalit' (oppressed).

Since then much has happened to labourers not only in the rural milieu but also in the urban setting. For one, the wall that is supposed to divide urban and rural, formal and informal, organised and unorganised labour has been shown up to have been nothing more than an illusion. The duality was questioned by Jan Breman and others and was demonstrated as being false; there is in fact a continuum between these various forms of labour in social, economic as well as political contexts. The bonded Musahar agricultural labourer in Purnea in Bihar is connected to the informal sector urban migrant worker in Ludhiana, seeking employment in one of the city's many hosiery factories. And the power-loom worker in Surat has members of his family toiling in the fields of Ganjam in Orissa.

Migration is one mode of establishing these connections. The huge mobility of labour in India belies the notion of the fixed, unchanging, self-sufficient village community. Every day millions of workers travel away from their homes in search of work and, of course, almost all Indian women — barring those in the small pockets of matrilineality that continue to exist in Meghalaya and Kerala — migrate at least once in their lives when they leave their natal homes after marriage. The intense and almost Brownian motion of workers in the Indian economy has not been checked either by the supposed tradition of immobility or by state action. Take for instance the Employment Guarantee Scheme in Maharashtra. It is one of the best devised schemes intended to provide employment to rural labourers within 20 kilometres of their homes. and thereby to stem the exodus from the countryside. While the scheme has indeed resulted in making the rural poor of Maharashtra less poor, it has by no means been able to stem the tide of migration either from the villages to the cities or from villages to other villages. Indeed the seasonal migration of sugarcane cutters from the villages of Khandesh in Maharashtra to south Gujarat has been documented by Jan Breman: it intensified precisely during this period as the expansion of irrigation expanded sugarcane cultivation.

But while there has been at least some state action with regard to rural labourers in Maharashtra through the EGS, in Kerala in the form of the Agricultural Labour Act and in West Bengal through Operation Barga, by and large it has been absent in the rest of the country. This is despite the evidence of acute distress in the drought-prone areas of Orissa, the devastation caused by the operation of market forces among cotton growers in Andhra Pradesh and the oppression by upper and intermediate caste landowners on *Dalit* landless workers in Bihar and elsewhere. The state appears to have abdicated its role in most of rural India *vis-à-vis* landless labourers.

The absence — or ineffectual presence — is even more evident in the context of non-agricultural rural workers. Whether it is among workers toiling in the stone quarries or children employed in carpet and *durrie* weaving units, among salt-pan workers or in brick kilns, among sand dredgers or road-builders — the awesome might of the state and its paraphernalia of laws and regulations is conspicuous more by its acts of omission than those of commission.

But the state is also largely absent among urban informal sector workers. Not only are people like rag-pickers and domestic servants, headload carriers and cart-pullers, artisans engaged in petty crafts production and vendors of goods in the streets, generally outside the purview of the state but so are most road repairers and construction workers who toil in the open air under the scorching sun or pouring rain, tinkers and tailors who work in the streets and in their homes, even goldsmiths and diamond polishers who sweat in dingy little workshops to produce glittering jewellery and glinting gems for the global market. If the state does make its appearance among them, it is mostly only to establish its majesty by enforcing 'law and order' and in the form of the extortionate inspector who causes more distress than he can alleviate. The withdrawal of the state, under the cover of the ideology of liberalisation, from its proactive social role and from affirmative action has also been accompanied by calls for the implementation of 'labour reforms' whereby exit policies are put in place to push more and more workers out of the sector where there are at least some securities offered by unionisation. The closure of composite textile mill after mill and the transfer of production to powerlooms have added to the vulnerability of labour as the state, like Pontius Pilate, washes its hands off.

Meanwhile, trade unions too are unable to significantly affect the lives of such workers. The national federations — and their number is legion — have been busy in the relatively easy industrial sectors of public and private enterprises. Charges of economism and fostering labour aristocracies have not succeeded in moving the major trade unions out of what is known, perhaps with deliberate irony, as the 'organised sector'. Organising blue-collar workers in secure jobs and moving on from there to unionising white-collar employees mostly in banks, government and other similar employment has kept labour leaders in business. And when blue-collar and white-collar workers are so important for them, they have no time for workers whose tattered rags have no collars at all!

But while trade unions and the state are generally absent from the lives of such labouring poor, capital is ever present. Indeed, the very existence and continuation of such miserable, exploited, oppressed labourers are essential to the forms of production that are increasing. More and more, the factory system — which in many ways aided organisation into trade unions — is being replaced by a new mode of operation of manufactories, 'putting out', and small-scale artisanal production. While the market for goods expands and intensifies, the market for labour expands only through migration and misery.

It is in fact the expansion and proliferation of the market for goods and services — globalisation, no less — which offsets the conditions of labour. The political economy of capitalism, analysed in the nineteenth century, was premised on the proletarianisation of labour but also, inevitably, on its organisation too. It was on that basis that there was prognostication of a time when 'expropriators would be expropriated' and there would be a transition to a social system whose guiding principles would be 'from each according to ability; to each according to need'. It was also the foundation of the establishment of the welfare state, of the trickling down of the benefits of increased social prosperity to those who constitute the base of society itself. In the conditions of the globalised market, of capitalism at the turn of the millennium, such egalitarian concerns are taken to be passé. These are times for the reassertion of the 'animal spirits' of aggressive consumerism, not for weepy sentimentality which contests what are seen to be the 'established truths of Social Darwinism': the fittest survive and the devil takes the hindmost. And yet, even the political economy of globalisation — cruel as it is — makes it clear that things are not as simple as that. The repeated invocation of 'comparative advantage' — in other less elaborate words, the use of poverty, backwardness, lack of organisation, low wages through intensified exploitation for 'value-addition' or subsidisation of costs of production — is clear indication that these factors of production which characterise the informal sector are not incidental but essential to contemporary, global capital.

In fact, there is an increasing tendency around the world, as in India, for greater casualisation, informalisation and contractualisation of labour. There is less need this way to employ labour on a regular basis and under regulated conditions. It is not only new technologies and new work processes that have made it possible to break up production in such a manner as to give parts of it out; even fairly old production systems have now been adapted to 'putting out' modes for which the currently fashionable jargon is 'out-sourcing'. Thus, payment by piece-rate is replacing payment by time rate in a manner that is almost a throwback to the 'pre-industrial' mercantilist age. This in turn means erosion of one of the major gains of labour: regulated working hours, the eight-hour working day, and the six-day working week. The casual, often home-based, worker is forced to extend the working day and sacrifice more and more of 'leisure' to service capital. In that respect, post-industrialism both borrows from and mimics pre-industrialism.

The result is that it is not even possible to apply scientific demography, one of the tools of modernity, to enumerate various segments of the workforce and to get reasonably accurate estimates of the numbers of workers in the informal sector. Such projections as are made are often based on exclusion: take the total working population — estimated to be around 330 million — and subtract from it the numbers of workers counted in the formal sector — estimated to be about 25 million — to arrive at an approximate number of workers in the informal sector. These include those engaged in agriculture, non-agricultural rural work as well as those in semi-urban and urban manufacturing as well as service sectors.

What is definitely known on the basis of fairly accurate statistics is that the rate of growth of formal employment has not kept pace even with the rate of growth of the Gross Domestic Product (GDP). When in the bad old days the GDP grew at the 'Hindu rate' of 3 to 3.5 per cent, employment grew only at 1.5 per cent. That was blamed on the dirigiste regime, statism, over-regulation. However, even in the era of de-regulation and liberalisation, when the GDP has been growing at rates between 6 to 8 per cent, the rate of growth of employment has not exceeded 2.5 per cent with 'salaried employment' actually registering a decline. Thus, quite obviously, more and more production is being carried out in the informal sector and more and more workers are being forced to seek 'jobs' — as distinct from 'employment' — in a sector where hours of work are long, returns on labour are low and living conditions are abysmal.

One of the consequences of this is that there is a fragmentation of labour itself and a segmentation of the working class, phenomena that have serious implications for the forms of mobilisation and organisation of the working class. The dispersal of workers from factory-based concentrations makes trade union activity that much more difficult since it reverses the socialisation processes that have been going on for a century or more. It prevents collective bargaining and reduces the possibility of work-based collective protest action.

These were not apparent to us when we were engaged in the Rural Labour Camp at Banmankhi. That was still the period when heroic collective effort was thought to be the mode to change societies. Shortly after the Camp, the Emergency regime, for instance, was thrown out by a mass democratic upsurge. Subsequently, during the 1980s, civil liberties and democratic rights movements, trade union campaigns, what were called 'non-party political organisations', parliamentary lobbying, even some judicial activism highlighted issues relating to bonded labour, child servitude, retrenchments and lay-offs, factory closures and lock-outs. It appeared that the answers to the problems created by capital were indeed to be found in the realm of civil society. It was possible, therefore, to stress the effectiveness of articulation and the importance of organisation in Rural Labour Camps and other such gatherings.

The last decade of the twentieth century has brought about change in this regard. Not only have changes in the organisation of work made Labour more vulnerable *vis-à-vis* capital but it has also put the two in different domains altogether. A significant aspect of the economic restructuring which has manifested itself in the 1990s is that while it has globalised capital — making it footloose, fancy-free and free-flowing across industries, sectors and even nations — it has made labour much more 'local'. This is despite its apparent mobility: the fact is that the reorganisation of work has made labour more insecure and, therefore, dependent on resources within the family, locality and the specific ecology of its habitat. The fact that there has been no sustained demand for the free flow of labour, without visa restrictions, across international boundaries to correspond to the transnationalisation of capital is one indication of this phenomenon of down and out localised labour serving global capital.

It is a gloomy scenario, one of exclusion of a large section of the people from the fruits of productivity to which they contribute. And yet, not only work but life itself must go on and dignity and hope, protest and resistance, honour and optimism must be asserted even in these dismal conditions. And they are. The forms of such assertion may not be dramatic; they may not be based on collective solidarity; they may have a mundane everyday quality; their locus may be the habitat, the home, the locality; the resisters and protestors may relate to each other as neighbours rather than as co-workers — nevertheless, protests and resistance go on and mobilisation and organisation are carried out in different ways. As Galileo said in another context, 'And yet it moves.'